The Romford Pelé

RAY PARLOUR

with Amy Lawrence

CENTURY

5 7 9 10 8 6 4

Century
20 Vauxhall Bridge Road
London SW1V 2SA

Century is part of the Penguin Random House group of companies
whose addresses can be found at global.penguinrandomhouse.com

Penguin
Random House
UK

First published by Century in 2016

www.randomhouse.co.uk

A CIP catalogue record for this book is available from the British Library

ISBN (hardback) 9781780895048
ISBN (trade paperback) 9781780895055

Typeset in India by Thomson Digital Pvt Ltd, Noida, Delhi
Printed and bound in Great Britain by Clays Ltd, St Ives plc

Penguin Random House is committed to a sustainable future for our
business, our readers and our planet. This book is made from Forest
Stewardship Council® certified paper.

MIX
Paper from
responsible sources
FSC® C018179

This book is for
Mum, Dad, John, Jim and Jo,
and my beautiful children,
Charlotte, Frankie, Georgina, Taite and Scarlett

Contents

Foreword by Arsène Wenger

In my football career I have never come across anyone else quite like Ray. It's simple – everybody loved him. Honestly, I did not always understand his jokes because he spoke in cockney. Even if I didn't understand them everybody laughed.

He typified the English culture. The guys sometimes had one beer too many, they were not training fanatics. Sometimes Ray came in and you could see he had not had completely twelve hours sleep that night . . . Training was a cure to get what they had been doing before out of their system. Luckily the positives of that culture were much stronger than the negatives.

Ray was a survivor of that generation when football was changing. Why? First of all he was brave. You could imagine that if you were in the trenches with Ray then he would fight next to you. I respected that. Secondly, he was a much better football player than people think he was. For me, the regret I have for Ray is that he was never recognised for the quality of his game and was a bit ostracised in his international career. I kept him because he was a great football player, not only because he had a sense of humour.

He brought a unique quality to the team because he was always happy to be with other people. He was a happy soul every day. Most of the time when you are in the hotel, for example, for some you feel it is a burden. We all love to play football but we don't necessarily want to be around other people. With Ray it was the opposite. He liked to be in the middle of the guys. He always brings positive vibes in a group of people.

On the pitch he gave us balance, and it was a credit to him that he was important whether he played on the right or in the centre of midfield, where he was also extremely good. I will never forget a game we played at Inter Milan where he played central midfield with Edu and we were absolutely outstanding.

On the right he gave you everything going forward but defensively he was reliable as well. He protected Lee Dixon. They were a pair who lived together in that team for a long time. Even when Lee had a bad ankle, Ray helped him out.

He had strong physical qualities, which explains why he played twelve years at the top with Arsenal. He had fantastic stamina and as a manager you knew you could rely on that. Many times I didn't see him so much in the first half but I kept him on because I knew the longer the game lasted the more you would see him. He always had a strong second half. He was a train who could go at a certain pace – not electric but he could maintain high energy the whole game.

I didn't realise that Ray tops the all-time appearances list for Arsenal in the Premier League. That is unbelievable. He should be grateful that I always picked him!

Arsène Wenger,
Arsenal training ground, 2016

Preface

TIM LOVEJOY: Oh no. He's put him through. Oh, it's all right. It's only Ray Parlour . . .

BRADLEY WALSH: [leaps up] YESSSSSSS! It's gone in!

TIM LOVEJOY: Oh no [sobs].

BRADLEY WALSH: That is some goal! That is Ray Parlour! That is the goal of the season! That is a goal!

TIM LOVEJOY: [head in hands, slumping on the desk] Ohhhh.

BRADLEY WALSH: That is Ray Parlour! He has done it all season. He is one of the only players in the Arsenal squad that will shoot from outside of the area! It's 1–0 Arsenal! Chelsea, where are ya?

FANZONE COMMENTARY, Millennium Stadium, Cardiff, FA Cup final, 2002

I SUPPOSE if you asked any retired professional sportsman what he regarded as a golden time in his career, he would probably pick a special season or a series of matches he played in. He may choose a club he played for, possibly a tour he went on or a great tournament he won. I would pick five days. More specifically, five days in May 2002. From 4 May through to 8 May to be exact. Those five days seem to encapsulate both my career and my lifestyle and they were unforgettable. As good as it gets.

BY THE start of May we were very close to winning the Premier League. We could clinch the title with our next fixture, at Old Trafford, against our arch rivals Manchester United. But before that we faced a very strong Chelsea side in the FA Cup final.

The cup final had been a special day in our household dating back to boyhood. It was always a big occasion, my dad would have his can of beer, all three boys – my brothers John, Jim and me – would have their orange juice, my mum would make everybody sandwiches, shut the curtains. The build-up was the best bit. As a kid, you would look at it and think: this is unbelievable. The players getting on the coach, having those big doors open up at Wembley, going out in a suit to look at the pitch, it was brilliant. That was easily our favourite time of the year.

Cup final always seemed to be boiling hot, curtains drawn, pitch-black, crowded round the TV, and we loved every minute of it. Three boys sitting there, completely gripped.

Saturday 4 May 2002. The Millennium Stadium, Cardiff. Arsenal v Chelsea. It had been a tough game, closely balanced, no breakthrough until the seventieth minute. I remember picking the ball up, it was a great pass from Sylvain Wiltord, but instead of having to face a player or two from Chelsea coming to tackle me, they kept backing off. It gets to a stage where they are retreating and you think: Jesus, I am getting closer and closer to the 18-yard box. Patrick Vieira and Sylvain made runs on the outside and it was expected I would pass to one of them rather than have a go myself. Those runs dragged two Chelsea defenders away from me. I remember dropping my shoulder.

It's one of those things you do a lot in training, but rarely in such a big game. Marcel Desailly turned his back a bit, he didn't dive at me or tackle me. He just let me shoot. I hit it. There are times when it comes off your foot and you know it is going in. There is no doubt in your mind you have hit the sweet spot. It's perfect. The right height, the right trajectory, the right swerve. Carlo Cudicini just got fingertips to it. Unstoppable though! It was probably the greatest moment of my life.

It was right in front of the Arsenal fans as well, which made it even better. There is a picture taken from behind the goal that shows the ball going in the net and the whole of the other end is blue. Freddie Ljungberg scored a spectacular goal ten minutes after mine and then Chelsea were gone. It was celebration time.

I was absolutely buzzing afterwards. Traditionally the FA Cup is the final act of the season but, weirdly, it wasn't this time. That wasn't going to stop me from going out to celebrate, even though there was the small matter of a couple more critical Premier League games. On the Wednesday night Arsenal were away to Manchester United. Win that and we win the double.

We flew back from Cardiff on Saturday evening after the FA Cup final and as the stewardess walked down the aisle of the plane I asked her for a beer. I was just about to take a sip when Arsène Wenger appeared and said, 'No drinking.'

'What, Boss? I've just scored in the cup final!'

'No drinking. Big game Wednesday at Old Trafford.'

'But, Boss, that's four days away. I'll be fine by then.'

'No drinking, Ray.'

I ended up slipping off to the back of the plane where my mum and dad and my brothers were. I said, 'Give me one of your beers, Jimmy.' I was just about to take a sip, but Arsène, who had walked all the way to the back of the plane, caught me before I got a taste. 'If I see you drinking, that's a fine of a week's wages.' Hmmm, £30,000 for one beer? I decided that was a bit much, so I gave it back to Jimmy.

That night I had a restaurant booked in Upminster. I was dating a new girl, Joanne, who had come to the cup final and I was taking her out to celebrate. Win or lose I was going. You have got to have something to eat.

I walked into the restaurant and it was full of Arsenal fans. Champagne was popping, then the tequila slammers started. I was dehydrated from the game, which accelerated the effects. In the end I was so drunk I stumbled out, falling over three tables.

Sunday morning. The day after a game we would have a warm-down. I went into training after a really nice sleep. I headed to the gym area, where all the mats were out for a forty-minute stretching routine – then we'd get a massage. After that you can go home. I sort of did my stretches, more or less lying around on the mat, stinking of alcohol, and decided to skip the massage. I couldn't be bothered with that. All the lads asked, 'Were you out last night?' I told them I was but I was fine. I left before Arsène came in so he hadn't seen me, which was probably just as well.

On the way home to my mum and dad's house I went past the Rush Green Social Club and knew my brothers were there, so I thought I would pop in to say hello. It's a great place, which reminds me of *Phoenix Nights*. From the front, with these frosted windows, you can't see in it, but inside is a massive bar. What makes it is the characters in there, like the old boy who drives his bike there and rides home swerving later on. There are all sorts, old and young. Dads go and then it gets passed down the generations to their sons. It's an old saying but it's all about who you are with, not where you are. It's brilliant. Tony Adams was always in there, Steve Bould and Wrighty and even Marc Overmars went in from time to time. It was £2 a pint, and it went without saying that whatever happened in that club stayed in the club.

I walked into a wave of happy faces and congratulations. As I am local most of them had backed me as first goalscorer, odds of 20/1. Someone had put a bet on 2–0 with me scoring at 100/1. Everyone was thrilled. 'Come on, have a beer,' they all said. I tried to explain: 'Seriously, I got really drunk last night, we have a massive game on Wednesday. Just one and I am off.' Next thing I knew I had downed ten pints of Guinness. No word of a lie. I was hammered.

I played the game at Old Trafford and we all put absolutely everything into it. I played really well, energetic, full of tackles and determination. Afterwards Martin Keown told me it was the best performance, defensively, that he had ever seen me put in. The way we chased and tackled and stood up to Man United in front of the back four that night was special. They were desperate to beat us. The last thing they wanted was to hand the title over to us in their own ground. They were brutal. Sylvain Wiltord scored the clinching goal and there was no way we would let United back in. We felt so powerful. We were champions. Double-winners.

Walking down the tunnel, we were all celebrating and I was pulled aside as they had awarded me Man of the Match. Sky came to fetch me for the interview, and they gave me this gigantic bottle of champagne, which symbolised this incredible moment in my career. I stopped for a second to try to take it all in. What a stunning week I have had. This is beyond belief. I felt so full of myself, walking back to the dressing room with this champagne, and the next minute Arsène Wenger taps me on the shoulder and says, 'I want a word with you, Ray.'

Oh no . . . I was thinking that someone from that restaurant had landed me in it. The club used to get loads of letters, people writing in saying where they had seen us and what we had been up to. I braced myself.

Arsène pulled me over and said, 'You were fantastic tonight, absolutely brilliant.'

1

George Graham's Tank Top

I once got suspended from school because of football. I went to Marshalls Park, in Romford. It wasn't a great school. The lads couldn't wait for lunchtime. It would be 10 v 10, out on the field. We didn't bother eating our lunch. We always played winning goal, which meant we had to keep going until we had a winner. So when the bell went, if it was 1–1 the lads were never going to stop. Five minutes into the next lesson, all the girls would be sitting in the classroom and all the boys were still out haring around in search of the winning goal.

One lunch we must have really pushed it, because the next assembly there was a big announcement. No more football. It was banned from the whole school. We wondered: what are we going to do now? We weren't allowed to bring footballs in any more. One day a few of us broke into the gym to have a five-a-side at lunchtime. We weren't doing any harm. We weren't running around plastering graffiti on things or causing damage. We just wanted to play football as we loved it so much. We realised we couldn't be seen in there but felt it was worth the risk. We got caught. The headmaster got involved. The next minute, everybody was suspended.

My mum wasn't too upset. 'At least you haven't done anything really bad,' she said. I remember the day she came up to school to see my head teacher. I was sitting outside the headmaster's office, aged fourteen or fifteen. It's a dodgy age, with the boys getting bigger and bigger and more difficult to control. As we were waiting to see the head, a teacher got pushed out of a nearby classroom. He was shouting, 'Let me back in!'

I turned to my mum. 'That's my class. I should be in there.'

She looked at me. 'You've got no hope in this school, have you?'

'Not really, Mum.'

That experience made me focus on wanting to be a footballer even more. I never had anything to fall back on. The first thing I say to kids now when I pay a visit to a school or youth club is: make sure you do your schoolwork. If you get an opportunity, practise football: don't go on your Playstation, go to the park or find a wall, wherever you can to try to have a kickaround – but always do your schoolwork as well. I got lucky. How many kids who want to be a footballer make it? If I hadn't made it in football, I didn't have any trade to fall back on. I don't know what I would have done. I would have found something, but I have no idea what.

Growing up in Romford, I was the youngest of three brothers born to my dad, Dave, and my mum, Ann. Being sporty was a major part of life for as far back as I can remember. We were always a very active family. Back in those days we were always going to holiday camps, Butlins, swimming, swinging golf clubs and, of course, plenty of football. Playing with my older brothers, I was always trying to beat them. I think that was good for me. The mix of a competitive streak and a sporty upbringing makes you stronger.

My brothers were always out playing football. My oldest brother, John, was very good. The middle brother, Jimmy, always used to say he was a better player than me. Everywhere we used to go and I was with him, he'd start: 'I'm a better footballer than him!' Later on when we were older and went out I would tell people, 'I'm a better taxi driver than him!'

On weekends or during the school holidays we'd always have a football. We'd go over to the park, my mum wouldn't see us for hours and hours, and usually I'd only come home when I was hungry. St Edward's School was just round the corner. They had a great wall there that you could hit the ball against non-stop, and we'd be there playing silly games all day, drawing circles on the wall to see who could kick the ball in the holes.

We'd sprint over to the field and make our own little Olympic Games. We had our own version of the Marathon: ten laps of our block, which was about five miles. My dad says I was running that non-stop at the age of six. The days went by in a flash. Before you know it, you are eating your dinner. I remember going out at nine o'clock in the morning, and I wouldn't be home until evening. Our parents didn't have to check up on us.

As a kid I was really quick. I held the sprint record over 80 metres at Hornchurch Stadium. The record was initially set in 1973, and I broke it roughly a decade later. Some years after that, when I was playing for Arsenal in my mid-twenties, this kid sent me a letter telling me that he'd beaten my record. So I wrote back to him to congratulate him and tell him I was proud my record had stood for a long time.

Because I was so quick when playing football I started out as a forward. I could score several goals each game just because I had the pace to outrun most opponents. Of course, it's easier at that age. You're playing against kids who aren't as fast, someone plays a ball in behind, the keepers were no good – bang! Then the stamina kicked in and it was obvious that that was my strength, so I moved more into midfield.

Playing with my older brothers and their mates really helped me. You can imagine: you're getting kicked a little bit more, getting rough-and-tumbled a bit more than if you were playing against guys your own age. I used to join and play in their little football matches and I always remember my brother John, who was four years older than me, telling my dad, 'Ray was running rings around all of my mates today.' I must have been about six at the time, so the other boys were giants compared to me.

Dad was proud. But there were no big ambitions about it. He'd always say, 'As long as he's having fun then that's all that matters.' My dad was very easy-go-lucky. He didn't really tell us off too much, but he always used to say to us that if you don't enjoy something, don't do it. He loved me going to football but he didn't want me going for the sake of it.

Believe it or not, where we used to play most of our football backed onto the West Ham training ground at Chadwell Heath. There is a big field there. It was amazing I never played for West Ham, to be honest with you. I was on their doorstep. We could see the training ground. My dad was a West Ham fan, he certainly would have encouraged me to go and train with them. But I never got asked.

My first live game was going to West Ham at Upton Park, in the Chicken Run. I was maybe seven or eight, and I remember standing up with my brothers. My dad saved up a lot of money for us to go, it was one of our birthdays but he took all three of us. We had the West Ham kit at Christmas.

My first club turned out to be Fulham. I signed for them when I was about nine years old. They actually came over to watch another player and noticed me playing for my Sunday team, Cloparcro. It was a newly formed club made out of three junior schools in the area – Clockhouse, Parklands and Crownfield. We played in the Echo League, a really competitive junior league in our area. It developed into an outstanding schoolboy team and we were Essex champions several times. Seven players who came out of that Cloparcro team went on to make their names as professionals. The others were Stuart Nethercott (who made it at Tottenham), Ty Gooden (Swindon), Dean Martin

(West Ham), John Cheesewright (Birmingham), Paul Reid (Wycombe) and Danny Warden (Charlton). My dad has been watching junior football for many years and says he has never seen a better schoolboy team.

One day this scout came over to watch another boy, but I had a really good game and he went over to my dad to ask if I would like to go and train with them. That was Fulham Football Club. We trained at Dagenham on a gravel pit and we learned so much. We absorbed a lot of football then, around eight or nine years old, which would be hugely beneficial later on.

I was just pleased to play football. In those days, I couldn't get enough of it. I don't think there was a single day when my mates knocked on my door and asked me if I wanted to have a kick about on the field, when I've ever said no. It was always: 'Yep, I'll be there in one second.' Trainers on, boots on, whatever, and out the door I sped. There was honestly nothing else to do. Nowadays kids have got everything, haven't they? Phones, iPads, all this technology. Back in those days all you had was football. We didn't have a lot of money either, my parents had normal jobs. My dad worked hard, he was a pipe-fitter. He used to go down the building sites. Then he ended up being a black cab driver towards the end of his working life. My mum did odd jobs and brought up the three boys.

As far as football was concerned, I reached a crossroads at the age of twelve or thirteen because I began to get into motocross, and it's obvious that, when you get to a certain level, football and motorbikes can't mix. A few of the lads in the area owned bikes. My brother Jimmy was right into it and we ended up sharing one.

Motocross was fun but I can't say I had a particular talent. I just loved the excitement – going fast, doing big jumps. It was dangerous, I don't know how my mum let me have a bike at twelve years old. If she'd seen what we used to get up to, she would've banned us on the spot. Luckily she wasn't about, she was at home, while we were in a field that at the time was probably illegal to bunk into.

I used to think to myself: do I want to go motocrossing or to football? At that point you don't really know what's next, you don't know what you want to do with your life. The decision became crystal-clear one day when I had a really bad accident. I hit a big stone and split my foot open. I needed stitches in my ankle. From that moment on I thought: that's it, I am never getting on a motorbike again.

After that incident was when I really told myself that I was going to start training hard and knuckle down. I had got into the habit of skipping training every now and again, I got a bit casual. You can't do that if you want to be

8

a footballer. If I was going to make a proper go of this, I would have to give it my full effort. I pinned my hopes on this idea that being a footballer was my future, so I put my head down and trained like mad.

At this point I was a young teenager trying to make the grade and suddenly there was a lot changing at Fulham. In 1987, there were plans afoot for the club to merge with QPR, to become Fulham Park Rangers. It never happened but a lot of the coaches at Fulham left during that period and there was an atmosphere of uncertainty. I liked Fulham. I liked the training, it was really enjoyable. But once the coaches left, I thought: that's it.

The timing was right to try my luck elsewhere. Steve Rowley was the scout who looked after the Essex area for Arsenal and he had been watching me for ages. He had spoken to my dad about me loads of times. Steve had brought Tony Adams to Arsenal, and Tony was in the first team at Highbury by then. Steve was so important for my early career, he really believed in me. When I got in trouble at school he used to go to see the headmaster on my behalf, and he kept encouraging me to make sure I made the best of the opportunity I had.

I went to Arsenal, and from the first moment I loved every single minute of it. To start with we trained at Grays, in a little indoor centre, and then in a school at Seven

Sisters. I would take the train there, walk a mile down the road to the school hall, where Pat Rice put us through our paces amongst all the gym equipment with apparatus tacked along the walls. The facilities were nothing special but we didn't care. I would walk back to the station, get on the train and go back to Barking station, where my dad would pick me up.

As we got older, we started going to Highbury. The sense of excitement really began to build. At the age of fourteen, Arsenal told me they wanted to sign me as an apprentice. That probably wasn't a good idea in that my schoolwork went out the window. I said to my mum, 'Look, Mum, I've got a job, I'm going to go and play football,' and I didn't turn up for school on some occasions, bunking off as usual. I wasn't doing anything bad, but I was just off down the park, dreaming about becoming a footballer. Somehow. I don't know how I'm going to do it, but I'm going to get there whatever it takes. That was my mentality really when I went into the apprenticeship.

Aged sixteen, we were at Arsenal every day, forty kids all together. It was dog-eat-dog. We had the likes of Andy Cole, who went on to be a great success with Manchester United and Newcastle amongst others, and Paul Dickov, who had a long and well-travelled career, in our group. It was proper, it got tough, and we all knew we would have to put the work in to make the all-important next step.

Life as a young apprentice was not all glamour. A sixteen-year-old at the Arsenal Academy today would not recognise too much of our daily routine. I would turn up at Romford station at around 6.30 in the morning. Arsenal would give you a little travel card for the week, at least they paid for your travel. I would get to either Stratford or Liverpool Street, then change to the Central line, then down to Holborn to catch the Piccadilly line to Arsenal.

We had to get to Highbury for eight o'clock, earlier if you were on kit duty. The apprentices were split into groups and we had different jobs that would rotate. It was the job of the apprentices to fetch the kit and load it up to be taken up to the training ground every day. In those days Tony Donnelly, the kitman, and his wife would bring the kit out, all nicely laid out from the wash the day before. We carried it all out in bundles to the little youth-team coach in Avenell Road, emblazoned with the Arsenal badge on the back, and threw it in the boot.

Once all the kit and all the boys were on the bus we'd go from Highbury all the way to London Colney in Hertfordshire. It would take about forty-five minutes to get there with all the traffic, so it would be about nine o'clock when we got there. Then we'd pile out, get all the kit out, and put it in the right places so the first team had their kit, the reserves had theirs, and so on.

We knew exactly where everybody sat and who needed what. Then we had to clean three pairs of boots a day, and we always had the same player to look after. We'd get their boots ready, make sure they were spick and span, and then obviously we had ourselves to take care of. So we'd all be getting changed, and then by this time the first team would be filtering in, the likes of Paul Davis, David O'Leary, Paul Merson, Steve Bould.

We didn't have a lot of banter with the first team, it would just be 'Oh, hello,' and stuff like that as we were too inhibited to try to get too friendly. But at Christmas time, the apprentices had to sing carols for the first team. Some of the lads would really be crapping themselves before they had to do it. You had to get on a big box in front of the entire first team and all the staff and you had to sing a song. No excuses. I remember getting on the box and singing 'Little Donkey'. It was around the time that Tony Adams used to get serenaded by opposition fans with hee-haw noises. I looked at Tony while I was singing my carol. He chased me all around the training field, threw a big bucket of water over my head. Some of the others were trying to sing properly but that was not for me. Leave off.

Youth-team training was challenging. The sessions were always difficult with Pat Rice as our manager. Pat was one who believed in working hard, and putting the maximum effort in.

Afterwards we had to look after all the boots that were left by the back door. We had to find our player's boots, clean them, put them all away – all in the freezing cold. Then, by that point, the first team had gone for lunch and dumped their kit on the floor, so we had to go in and tidy all that up as well. Some put it in bundles to make it easier for us, but most of them just lobbed it anywhere. We put everything into the laundry bags, put them back onto the coach and then we would have our lunch.

Late afternoon the coach would finally trundle back to Highbury with us and everyone's kit. Once we had unloaded and got it to Mrs Donnelly, that was your day. I'd walk another mile back to the station and get the train home. Having got started at six o'clock every morning, by the time I was back in Romford I had almost done a twelve-hour day. Only a small percentage of that was actual training.

On Fridays, we'd have to do our duties to prepare for matchday. A group of lads would take turns to clean out the bus, clean the dressing rooms, referee's room and so on. That was just part of the apprenticeship. En route to

Highbury we'd stop at the fish and chip shop and our lunch would be ready for us. We'd all go back and eat it in the dressing room before we started cleaning it. It's crazy thinking back now, but that's all we'd be doing before a game – cleaning and scrubbing. Comparing our experience to today's young players, it seems like bloody luxury now.

Pat Rice was quite the taskmaster. He used to come in and check on all of us to make sure we were doing it properly. He would run his finger along a surface to check. 'A bit of dust there, do it again,' he'd bark. But as annoying as it was, it built a good team spirit and he knew that. Naturally, some were lazier than others, and that came out in the future when it started getting serious. The lazy ones couldn't be bothered with the training.

We used to have a muck-about when we were cleaning out the dressing rooms. I mean, imagine it in the summer months, there were a few occasions when we would open the big windows at Highbury. You'd see a large group of people walking past along Avenell Road and of course we had the hose, and we used to pretend to clean the floors but we would angle it up to the windows and soak people. Sometimes they would come in complaining to Pat Rice, and we used to say, 'Oh, sorry, Boss, we were just trying to spray the wall, we didn't know anyone was walking past . . .' But he knew what we were really up to.

From day one, Pat Rice really drummed in what it meant to be an Arsenal player. I learned that early. After about a year playing for Arsenal, that was my club. I thought: this is the team I want to play for. That was down to Pat. That shirt became special to me every time I put it on.

You don't have a choice as a kid. I was taken to West Ham because my dad was a West Ham fan. But this was my choice. It was natural. I really loved the club and its ways. I remember going up to the marble halls when I was young and thinking: this is stunning. Going up those stairs for the first time and seeing the bust of Herbert Chapman, it just hit me. That class. Walking into those really old dressing rooms, feeling the fantastic history in the air, that was what it was all about. After that I looked up about Arsenal's past. My dad told me things he knew about the club and its players back in the day, people like Charlie George.

Pat used to tell us how important it was to play for this great club. He went through what we went through, as a young lad here himself, hoping to make it. What Arsenal did for him, he tried to explain to us, could happen to us. It could make a great life for you.

They were golden days, it just felt like you were with a group of mates playing football and enjoying plenty of laughs throughout the rest of the working day. As youngsters, we learned a lot from putting in all those hours, showing we were prepared to do what it takes. It was hard work, especially for kids our age, getting up at the crack of dawn and getting home in the evening barely having stopped. That made you really appreciate every opportunity you were given even more. When you got in the reserves, or the first team, you gave everything to try to crack it. You'd see the first team coming in, doing a bit of training, kicking a few balls around, dumping their kit on the floor and going home. You'd think to yourself – oh, I wish I was doing that – because everybody loved playing football. Nobody loved cleaning.

I remember when I first turned up as an apprentice, we had six or seven players at Arsenal who represented England at youth level. Some of us were still a bit raw, coming straight out of school, but we were always in awe of them, thinking: wow, they play for England, they must be amazing. I remember the likes of Mark Flatts, Steven Clements, Matthew Joseph, who all came from Lilleshall, the Football Association's School of Excellence.

I remember in training once, I smashed Steven Clements, who was the England captain at the time, and I said, 'Oh, sorry, I didn't mean that.' He looked at me and said, 'I'm the England captain, what are you tackling me like that for?' I was so sorry. All of a sudden, Pat Rice stopped the training, came over to us and I was thinking: oh, God,

I'm gonna get hammered here, because I really took him out. Pat went up to Clements and asked, 'What did you say?' and he said, 'Oh, I'm the England captain, you can't kick me like that.' Pat Rice said, 'You're not the England captain here,' and he told me to kick him harder next time. I thought: this is brilliant!

Next tackle – bang! Another tackle – bang! He really didn't like it, Clements, and he was supposedly going to be the best player by a mile out of all of us. I don't know what happened with him in the end. You can just see that some players have all the talent, but they just don't want it enough. Some terrific players take their eye off the ball a little bit, aren't focused, and it was amazing to see how many talented players didn't make it. Whereas I probably would have been about tenth down that list of the forty players and I made it.

It just shows you how hard it actually was to make it then, and that was without any foreign players, it was all British players. There were quite a few lads from Scotland in our group and we had plenty of banter between the Jocks and the cockneys. We had a fantastic team spirit. These days it is completely different, with young players from Spain, Italy, Brazil all in the youth team. The communication must be difficult at times. I really enjoyed the atmosphere. It was the period in my life when everything seemed bright.

As a youth player we played in the South East Counties League, a really competitive league on Saturday mornings. It wasn't uncommon to be having a good game and Pat Rice would substitute you – just as you were wondering why you had been taken off when you were playing well, he would tell you to get changed. 'Get back to Highbury, you are a sub for the reserves this afternoon.' You'd get changed, rush back to Highbury, put your kit back on and the next minute you are sitting behind the dugout for a Combination game, which was the reserve league – those matches would be played at our stadium when the first team were away. That was going up the ladder. Being sub for the reserves at Highbury was a real honour, that step closer to the biggest dream of all.

As for first-team games, we used to attend every match and would sit in the paddock, which was an area behind the dugout. So, if we had played a South East Counties game in the morning, we would grab some sandwiches from the canteen and head back to Highbury to get a taste of the real deal. I was drawn to this idea of playing in front of people, I could feel the atmosphere crackling. It made you want to play on that stage.

Apprentices got two tickets for each game as a perk. Our wages were £27.50 per week, with a bonus of £3 if we won our youth-team games. So most of the apprentices used to sell their tickets to make some extra. If you sold your tickets for £10 each, maybe a bit more for a big game, you could virtually double your money for the week. I used to sell a lot of tickets on behalf of the apprentices. The lads used to give me theirs, and I would take a big pile to a tout I knew who sold them for us.

The arrangement suited everybody. The youth-team players were happy because they were getting money in their pot and they didn't have to do anything. I used to gather the lads all round with my pockets full of money, and share it out between everyone. But I was earning a little bit extra on top for dealing with the tout so in those days I could boost my earnings to around £150 a week.

By the time all the tickets were sold we all had a few quid, no hassle, and we would go into Highbury feeling good and head for the Halfway House. That was a little room that was situated halfway down the narrow tunnel that led out to the pitch. We made sure we were all in our seats behind the dugout in time for the first team to come out. I just remember the atmosphere was electric and you couldn't help but wonder if hopefully one day it would be you running out in front of the old North Bank and Clock End.

The ticket scheme went on for ages. Most games, really. It was common practice in football. We loved it when there was a cup game at home, because we'd be able to price them for more than the usual league games. The apprentices seldom needed the tickets to use for themselves. All those from outside London, the boys from up north or Scotland, didn't have family or friends who were likely to go, so the ticket scene ended up being a nice earner coming in at the end of the week. It's just what everybody did.

I remember getting caught once. George Graham called me into his office. I was just a young kid. He told me that they were going to ban my tickets for the rest of the year!

Arsenal enjoyed some incredible times under George. He put together a young, hungry team and it made a big impression to witness that success. I was sixteen when Arsenal became English champions. Winning the First Division, as it was then called, becoming the top dog of football in our country, was thrilling. The way Arsenal did it, too, was with one of the most dramatic games I ever saw.

In 1989 they went to Anfield on the last game of the season, and needed to win by two clear goals to take the title from Liverpool. It was such a tight margin – goals scored would be decisive with both teams tied on points and goal difference. I watched the game at Romford dog track on the TV. My mum was working there at the time, taking bets. My brothers went that evening and I must have tagged along.

I remember watching the drama unfold. Arsenal were massive underdogs but Alan Smith scored the opening goal and the season went down to the last seconds, when Michael Thomas made it 2–0 in stoppage time. What that Arsenal team achieved that night for me goes down as the best result ever. People talk about the situation more recently when Sergio Agüero scored to give Manchester City the title in 2012, but that was against QPR, who were hovering around the relegation zone. In 1989 it was first versus second in a one-off duel.

As a young apprentice, obviously we felt proud of the club, but also it whetted the appetite even more to try to become a part of that first team. The opportunity didn't feel a million miles away. In those days you could see a pathway without a doubt. The average number of pros in each squad was smaller than nowadays. As an apprentice you had your eye on the reserves, and tried to figure out who was in front of you so you could step on his toes, try to match or even get ahead of what they were doing. The same targets presented themselves once you were in the reserves looking on at the first team. I wanted to crack it.

The first breakthrough came suddenly. I got the phone call at home. The phone call you always want. It was a

Friday night. 'Ray, we have had a player drop out unwell, you are in the squad.' I thought: what? Arsenal were playing away at Norwich. It wasn't long after my eighteenth birthday, towards the end of the 1990–91 season. Arsenal were top of the league, it was neck and neck with Liverpool during that run-in.

I got the train on my own up to Norwich, they told me exactly how to get there and someone picked me up from the station to take me to the team hotel. That train journey thoughts were swirling through my mind. Will I be on the bench? Will I get on? Will I play my first-ever game at eighteen years old?

When I got there, I looked out for Tony Adams, the most familiar face for me now I'd moved up with the big boys. I knew Tony as he was from my area, he only lived around the corner, and Steve Rowley had mentioned to Tony to keep an eye out for me coming through the ranks. 'This kid,' said Steve, 'he is a nightmare at school, he is causing havoc but he is going to be top player.' Tony helped me massively. I looked up to him as a kid of seventeen, eighteen. He was my role model. He was the one who took me under his wing.

As a youngster you don't even know where to sit or who you should sit with in new company like that. I caught up with him and said, 'Tone, I'm absolutely cacking myself here, what do you have to do?' He said, 'Dinner tonight, you have to stand up and do a speech. Every single player on their debut or their first-ever trip has to stand up and do a speech.'

'What do you have to say?'

'Well, just thank the manager, say something about the lads, how it's a real honour; you've been working hard in the youth team and now you've got your opportunity, you hope there are many more opportunities to come, just thank everybody. And whatever you do – I'll just give you a bit of advice – just mention something about the manager's clothes. He really likes that.'

'Cheers, Tone.'

I was grateful, thinking that it was good of him to tip me off and help me out. So, when we finish dinner, glasses tapping, I stand up, a bit nervous and start my speech.

'Boss, I'd just like to thank you very much for inviting me up here today, it's what I've dreamed of, travelling with the first team for my first game. To be with all these fantastic players, Dave Rocastle, David O'Leary, Tony Adams. It's a real honour to be here. I hope for a lot more opportunities and hopefully I can play well in the reserves and earn the chance to show you what I can do. Oh, and by the way, Boss, all the lads really like your tank top.'

George's face was a picture. 'Sit down, son,' he said.

All the players started laughing, because they know what George was like with his clothes. He always thought he looked the part, immaculate. So Tony Adams had stitched me up big time. Later, Tony told me he had only been joking and that I shouldn't really have said anything about his clothes. That was the first time I got into the banter with the first team.

The experience of travelling to Carrow Road was a big step. I thought I'd be the man left out. Anyway, it turned out I was sub and I'm thinking: oh no, this could be my debut . . . I remember just warming up was unbelievable, the fans close to the pitch and the noise of the place. We used to play for the reserves in front of 200 people so there was no noise. In front of a proper crowd, that's when it suddenly hits you. This is what I've really got to try and achieve here. I never got on in the end. I watched as we drew 0–0 and even though I didn't get on it was an exciting feeling to be part of it all.

It seems a couple of them already had an eye on my progress. The first team used to have bets on who would make it from the youths. They used to watch a few youth-team games here and there. As well as Tony keeping an eye out for me, Paul Merson had tipped me to be the player who came through. He told me, 'You are my tip for the top.' That was a boost coming from a player I admired.

Merse was an excellent player. He had to work hard to get where he got, he was considered too small at one stage and nearly left, but when he got his opportunity he was brilliant and had great flair going forward.

When I got to the first team, I roomed with Merse for a year. I got on really well with him, as I still do now. He was my first room-partner and we had some fun. It was brilliant, gambling every day. As soon as we got to the room Merse would find a dog race, on Channel 4, or even teletext in the old days.

He would ask me, 'Who do you fancy here?'

'Number four.'

'Why do you say that?'

'I don't know. You just asked me, so I just picked a number.'

He would get on the phone and have a bet. A few dogs we chose might win but usually by dinner time we had lost all our money. Merse was a great character and being with him was both hilarious and a nightmare. I ended up getting a gambling account. I gambled anyway. I had that in me from going to the dog track as a young kid, playing fruit machines. Merse was perfect for you if you liked a gamble.

As a young footballer trying to find my way in the early 1990s, what better guides than Paul Merson and Tony Adams showing me the ropes?

2

The Tuesday Club (and a Plant Pot for Christmas)

Being a protégé of Tony Adams allowed me to dip my toe into a lifestyle that was irresistible. I was in my late teens, just breaking into the first team, and I started going out locally in Essex whenever Tony gave the word. I was still living with my mum and dad. There was one infamous occasion when we went to Epping Forest Country Club, and I was chatting up this girl and giving it the big 'un. I asked her if she wanted to come back to my house, but obviously I didn't really have a house to invite her to. She said yes. I thought: oh no, what do I do now? I can't take her back to my mum and dad's.

I asked Tony if I could go back to his house with this girl and he said no problem and handed over his keys. I knew his address, we popped in a cab, driving past the beautiful houses, and she said, 'Oh, you are doing all right for yourself.' Tony's house had a swimming pool so I suggested we go back, have a swim in the back garden, then a few drinks . . . She seemed impressed.

We walked up the path, and I got the keys out, full of cocky confidence. 'Come on in!' As I opened the door, the alarm started beeping. Uh-oh. I take a guess and look under the stairs and luckily find the alarm. Now, what could the code be? I try everything. Tony's shirt number is six so I punch in 6666. Nope. 0000. Nope. 1111. Nope. I thought: it's Tony, it can't be too hard! I try pulling wires out of the thing to disconnect it. Next minute, the alarm siren is blasting. The system was wired up to the police for a quick response and within two minutes a police car turned up. They were firing questions at me. Is this your house? 'Yes . . . Well, not exactly.' Before I know it they've arrested me because they didn't know who I was.

I told them I was Tony's friend and tried phoning him, but Epping Forest Country Club is, as the name suggests, in the middle of a forest, so there was no reception. I can't get hold of Tony. I've been arrested, and this girl is about to be left stranded outside the house of someone she doesn't know. What a disaster.

Bizarrely the mother of Robert Lee, who had a fine career with Charlton and Newcastle, lived next door. Hearing the commotion, she came out in her dressing gown. She recognised me and intervened with the police, explaining she could vouch for me and that I played with Tony. They let me go.

Tony came home. I had done about £200 worth of damage to his alarm. He asked what on earth I had been doing, thinking pulling the wires out would help. I told him I was desperate to make it stop. He was fuming. It was very embarrassing for me.

The girl asked, 'Is this really your house?'

I owned up. 'I was only joking, it's my friend's house.'

She laughed. Amazingly I took her out again afterwards. I think she felt sorry for me!

Tony had the respect of everyone at Arsenal. Even as youth-team players we saw it when he trained. Sometimes the youth team would play against the first team on a Friday. You know you can't tackle them but you also know when you had the ball you had to make sure you put that bit extra in, show the manager that you can play for the first team one day. Tony took control and told us what to do. 'Just calm down, son, you know we've got a big game tomorrow and this is only shadow-play really, trying to get us into the correct positions.' Tony was always that leader. You could feel that whether you were a youth-team player or an experienced pro playing by his side. Tony was in charge of this team without a doubt. It meant a lot to me that we hit it off as I was just starting out.

Tony and David O'Leary had been room partners, but when it looked like David was coming towards the end of his career – he left Arsenal in 1993 after playing well over 700 games for the club – Tony took me aside and told me that the moment David left, I would be going in with him as his new room partner. We roomed together for almost ten years, until Tony retired.

The thing that really surprised me when I came into the team was the drinking culture. The first thing the players said to me is, 'You can come in the pub now. You're allowed, because you are in the squad.' I thought: that's good news. Don't get me wrong, it wasn't as if I had never been out. My brothers were in pubs from the age of fifteen or sixteen and I followed suit, so it was hardly a shock to the system. But it was more of a surprise because I expected that once I got into the first team I wouldn't be able to go out so much. As it turned out, we started going out even more. In a way – perhaps not everybody's way – I had the best football upbringing you could get, gambling with Merse and drinking with Tony.

The Tuesday Club, as it was known, was in full flow and I was soon welcomed into the fold. The Tuesday Club came about because in those days we used to train at Highbury on a Tuesday. If there was no midweek game we would be put through our paces, it was always a really intense session, and then have Wednesday off, before coming back in on Thursday to prepare for Saturday's game.

Tuesday training was a real physical day. There was a lot of hard running, up and down the terraces and round the pitch. But everybody always used to dress up to go in on a Tuesday. George would say, 'What's going on here?' It was obvious we were all going out after because our clobber would give the game away. Usually we'd be in our tracksuits Monday, Thursday and Friday. But on Tuesday we had all our gear on as if we were going for a night out. We'd leave Highbury and shoot down the road heading for Covent Garden or, more locally in Islington, Upper Street – or wherever in town the mood took us, as we knew we had Wednesday free to recover.

Quite a few of the lads went out drinking as that was a perfectly accepted part of the football lifestyle. By the tail end of the George Graham era, Tony Adams, Bouldy and Merse were amongst the hard core. Nigel Winterburn and Alan Smith would come out now and again. In 1994 Arsenal signed this player from Denmark, John Jensen, and when he turned up he explained his nickname was Faxe, which was the name of a Danish beer. He had been awarded his nickname because he had the reputation of being a big drinker back home. Well, the lads took him out for the first time and that night he ended up comatose. After six pints he was on the floor. He said, 'I can't believe you lot drink as much as you do.'

It was great for team spirit and everybody knew we still had to work hard, which we did. Training-wise you'd have a good sweat-up and get it out of you quickly if you'd had a booze-up. The socialising and the football went hand in hand.

It was a regular thing. To be fair I think every club had their own version of the Tuesday Club in those days. And the team spirit was stronger for it. Sometimes we had the whole team out, which was great because we would be in the pubs together, mixing, and sometimes we would talk about football but also we would talk about normal things in life, what was happening with the girlfriends and wives. It was really an eye-opener from the first time I went out with them and I couldn't get enough of it, I loved it. I couldn't wait for Tuesday – a serious running session, straight down the pub, the classic work-hard, play-hard mentality.

The drinking was fairly relentless. Saturday night after a game, then Sunday afternoon was the best drink of the week, usually in the pub down our way. Monday we might have a couple after training, then came the Tuesday Club . . . We were probably drinking too much but the enjoyment of it, and just being around Tony at that time, was far too much fun to turn down. If Tony said, 'I'm going out,' I was like a little puppy jumping along after him. 'I'll come with you, Tony, definitely.'

It sounds daft but those sorts of days were fantastic. I once had Tony and Steve Bould in the back of my car driving around north London, and whenever we got to a mini-roundabout, if nobody was coming I would drive straight over it. We took off, like the Dukes of Hazzard and, with two big six-foot-somethings in the back, their heads went bang against the roof of this little car. When I returned the car, eventually, the dealer said, 'What are these two head marks in the back of this car?'

'Oh, yes, that's Tony Adams and Steve Bould.'

I remember going out on Christmas Eve once and – not unusually for us – doing something foolish, because at that time of life you think more about the larks than any trouble it might lead to. It was my first full season, and neither Tony nor myself was in the squad for the Boxing Day game, so we headed out in the afternoon after training. We settled down for a drink in the Palms Hotel, which is near us in Romford, and I said, 'Tony, whatever we do I have to get my mum a present for Christmas.'

'No problem, Ray. We have got plenty of time. We can have a few beers and then we will have a look and see what we can get.'

We stayed in there all afternoon and forgot all about it. It got to the stage where it was early evening, Christmas Eve, all the shops were closing. Suddenly the thought popped back into my head.

'Tony! The present! What are we going to do now?'

He looked at me. 'I don't know . . .'

We were standing next to a plant pot and he said, 'What about this? Will that be all right?' We weren't really thinking what we were doing, so we picked up this plant pot and put it in the boot of my car. The manager of the hotel saw us walk out with it, not that we noticed. We went back in and had a few drinks. 'Nice one, Tony,' I said. 'She will be happy with that.'

When we left Palms the police were waiting by my car. They asked me to open up the boot. I tried to wriggle out of it. 'Oh, I've given my keys to someone and they must have mucked about and put something in there.' The policeman said, 'No, the manager of the hotel saw you and Tony Adams walk out of the hotel with this plant pot and put it in the back of your car.' I thought: oh no . . . I took the plant pot back to the hotel and helped them to lift it into its rightful place.

Tony and I had to go to the police station the following Tuesday. I told Tony on the way to training. Believe it or not, as we walked in the policeman tooted, 'Here comes Bill and Ben.' The flower pot men. Top marks there. Fortunately, once we had taken the plant pot back and apologised the hotel let us off. They could have pressed charges but it was kept quiet and didn't even make the papers. We were young, we were enjoying ourselves, taking chances, and not really thinking about the consequences. The culture in football made it too easy to have a few drinks and end up wavering on the borderline of what was acceptable behaviour-wise.

Our manager, George Graham, had been a rogue as a player. He had the nickname of 'Stroller' and earned a reputation for enjoying a good social life. But it seemed he tried to do the opposite as a manager. He wanted us to go out and have a few beers here and there, but he was not keen on anyone stepping out of line. He wanted to keep an eye on us.

One Tuesday he couldn't work out where we were going and it transpired he sent out one of his spies to try to track us. In London you can get lost so easily. One particular week we were going to a bar called Champions in Southgate, and we didn't realise we were being followed. Stewart

Houston was George Graham's mate and his assistant manager, and had been trailing us from a car a distance behind.

We were all sitting there in the bar. There was a reserve game coming up, and some of the squad were due to be playing. You really shouldn't be out if you've got a reserve game. I wasn't playing in the reserves so I was okay.

I was sitting at the front window of Champions and for some reason I turned round and looked outside at the exact moment Stewart Houston walked past. He was trying not to be too obvious as he peered through the window. He didn't come in, he just wanted to see who was in there so he could report back to the manager.

I said, 'Lads, I've had a few beers but I'm sure that's Stewart Houston by that window.' Some of the lads who were due to play in the reserves went '*What?*' and plonked down their beer to run out the back door. George would have fined them a week's wages if he found out they were in a pub before a reserve game. Stewart Houston had to walk back past the window to get back to his car in the car park. So the remaining players all stood by the window having a drink and, after a few minutes, there he was returning past the window to see us all staring back at him. By this time all the reserves had gone. We beckoned him in.

'All right, Stew?'

'Sorry, lads, the boss made me follow you to see what you are getting up to.'

George couldn't work out the Tuesday Club at the time. He knew a few of us were off out but the details were not under his control. The players were wary of George, but Tony could get away with almost anything as far as the manager was concerned.

I remember once all the lads were moaning about bonuses, as I don't think the money had changed since the 1970s. They all asked Tony to say something to George, and one day he was in the manager's office for at least an hour, supposedly talking about that very thing. The lads thought this was a good sign. Tony came out and the lads asked, 'Well, what did you get for us, Tone?'

He just smiled. 'We didn't get a change in the bonuses but I got a new four-year contract.' George just loved Tony, he really respected him as a skipper and knew the qualities and the desire he had.

Looking back, it was a massive shock to everyone at the club when Tony got sentenced for drink-driving in 1990. I was seventeen at the time. The incident happened near to where I lived, and the captain of Arsenal, the man I looked up to, was on the front page of the newspapers for crashing his car through somebody's wall. They made an example of him when they sent him to prison. It was just before Christmas when he went to court, and it was obvious it would make huge headlines that would warn about the consequences of drink-driving. He was sentenced to four months in prison.

He served half his sentence and was released, and I was in the paddock watching when he played his first game back at Highbury. It was a reserve match against Reading. Absolutely thousands of fans came to see Tony, even though the first team were playing at the exact same time that afternoon in an FA Cup replay at Leeds. The crowd was massive, we had never seen anything like it. Most of the reserve team that day were the players I had grown up with in the youth side. And there was Tony, back in the fold. He was as skinny as anything.

Later, when I got in the first team and we became room partners, I talked to him about that experience. He was always very open with me. When he got to Chelmsford prison they asked him after a while if he wanted to go to an open prison instead but he said he was fine where he was. He had found his place in that environment. He could go to the gym when he wanted, run around the perimeter when he wanted, and he got left alone in there. The main man inside had told Tony that if anyone picked on him to tell him and it would get sorted out. That was it. He was left to manage the situation. The way he handled that episode was Tony through and through. He figured out what he wanted, which was to keep himself to himself and keep fit. He didn't see the point of moving to an open prison. He decided to do his sentence, that's it.

Before long he was back in the team for the remainder of the season, and Arsenal finished that extraordinary 1990–91 campaign as league champions. They had to overcome adversity – as well as missing their captain for a while the FA docked the club two points for a brawl in a feisty game up at Old Trafford – but George Graham was good at creating a siege mentality. I suppose we needed it.

After his drink-driving episode, I was quite often Tony's driver. We lived close by and I would often take him to training. I had a Mini Metro, and how he, a big centre-half, got into that I will never know. We once broke down on the M25. I was worried, as George Graham would hand out an instant £50 fine if you were late for training. Tony ended up pushing my car down the hard shoulder of the motorway, trying to jump-start it. He was the England captain but he didn't mind.

Once we went out after training into central London. 'Shall we have a couple of drinks in town today?' Tony asked.

'Yeah, no problem, I've got my car,' I replied and off we drove to Moorgate. I left the Mini Metro in a car park there, and by the time we had downed a few pints there was no way I could drive home so we left the car and took a cab back to Essex.

'How are we going to get to training tomorrow, Tony?'

'No problem, I'll book a cab to pick us up and take us to training, after that we can go and fetch your car from Moorgate.'

So we went to training, returned to Moorgate and, as I was about to collect my car, Tony said, 'That was a great day at the pub yesterday, shall we go back for a pint before we head off?' Several pints later, I looked at Tony. 'Can't drive again, Tone.' The routine repeated and my little Mini Metro ended up in that car park for three days running. We kept going to pick it up and ended up sidetracked by the pub. We had a cab driver from Essex who did the round trip with us on a few occasions. He loved Tony so he gave us a discount.

Off-field diversions cropped up fairly frequently, and Tony and I found ourselves in the thick of one that turned sour in 1993 with an incident concerning a fire extinguisher which ended up plastered all over the newspapers.

We had been drinking one afternoon at the Chequers, a little pub in Hornchurch that was Tony's local. We were hungry and decided to go for something to eat. We ended up in a Pizza Hut in Hornchurch. We were minding our own business when all of a sudden some Tottenham fans walked in and they sat there with their girlfriends and soon began to mouth off.

I wasn't a big player then, I was only beginning to get my first few opportunities, but the experience proved to me how much more difficult it is to have a normal life and do normal things when you become a household name. I couldn't believe what these people were doing to Tony. I was gobsmacked. They were throwing carrots from their meal, calling him a 'donkey', loudly and obnoxiously talking amongst their table, 'Do you know what a donkey is?' and all giving it the big 'un. They were showing off to their girlfriends really.

I said, 'Tony, how do you put up with it?' There were probably four blokes to be fair and he said, 'Don't worry about it, Ray, I've got used to it.' The donkey jibes had started quite a few years before, in 1989, when Tony played in a massive game between Manchester United and Arsenal at Old Trafford. It was pouring and muddy and intense and Tony scored a brave header to put Arsenal in front, then was unlucky to score an own goal which sliced off his boot in the rain and allowed United to equalise. The following day the *Daily Mirror* printed his picture with a pair of donkey ears superimposed. Some opposition supporters used to throw carrots towards him on the pitch.

It was a bit much to see people in a restaurant having a go when we were only having a meal. 'It doesn't bother me,' he said. But these Tottenham fans kept going on and on. 'Tony, this is an absolute joke,' I said. I noticed there was a fire extinguisher right next to our table. 'Tone, pull that pin, I want to sort them out.'

'All right, then.'

In that split-second the mood was transformed. He pulled the pin and I picked up this fire extinguisher and, as I went to spray it, it was so powerful that it went over my head. I couldn't get control of it, I sprayed the whole lot everywhere. The pictures were coming off the walls, chairs tipping over, all their pizzas got drenched and everything. I promise you, I soaked them properly. We had paid the bill already, so I put the fire extinguisher back on the stand and we walked out. A couple of other diners were laughing and said, 'They deserved that,' as we left.

One guy who was having a meal did not take it so well and chased us. As he got to Tony, he looked at Tony and saw the size of him and you could see him suddenly change his tune. He retreated back to the restaurant without saying anything.

We ended up going to a little social club around the corner just to go and hide out for a bit. So we had a few more drinks. We went back to Tony's house and believe it or not we decided more food was a good idea. We were starving again and phoned for a Chinese takeaway. A moment after that was delivered, a police car arrived at Tony's house. A policeman knocked on the door and I went to answer it, with a bag of Chinese food still in my hand. 'Were you involved in an incident with a fire extinguisher that was sprayed at Pizza Hut?' asked the officer.

'No, no, look I've got a Chinese right here.'

'So you haven't been at Pizza Hut in Hornchurch today?'

'Well . . . I was in there earlier . . .'

We ended up being cautioned and really didn't know what to expect in terms of whether there would be any repercussions. I was prepared to pay for the damage at Pizza Hut. I didn't mind that. But we hoped that that might be that and we would get away with it.

Tony phoned me on the Friday night. 'We are right in it now.'

'What's happening, Tone?'

'We are on the front page of the tabloids tomorrow morning.'

'Oh, no, George Graham is going to go mad.' I was thinking: I don't need this. But we couldn't avoid the inevitable.

Saturday morning, I made my way to the pre-match meal at South Herts Golf Club. All the rest of the lads had seen the paper. George pulled us aside for a word. 'I want to see you after the game today, both of you.' I remember the game. We drew 0–0 against Man City. Afterwards we got changed and Tony and I made our way upstairs through the marble halls to where George had his office. He began to tell us off and wanted an explanation.

Tony began to talk and, wanting to do me a favour as a young kid, he tried to shoulder the blame and say he had been spraying the fire extinguisher. 'We got a bit frustrated and I sprayed them,' he said.

'All right, Tony,' said George. 'I understand. See you at training Monday morning.'

Then he turned to me. 'Two weeks' wages.'

'*What?*'

'For getting yourself in the paper it is a two-week fine. I know it was you.'

So Tony walked out with nothing. Not even a fine. George would never tell Tony off. Tony was his man. I had to cough up £700 as I was on £350 a week. Later Tony asked me how much my wages were and he gave me half the money for the fine.

In fairness, by fining me George was probably trying to teach me a lesson, give me a jolt. It might seem like a great story now, it was funny, and it was for the right reasons, but it was a bad dream at the time. You know you shouldn't be provoked but there are limits. Tony's dad was furious with him. I told him I had done it, I was sticking up for Tony. Sometimes you can't let people get away with hassling you.

Overall, George was great for my career. He always pushed me. I think you needed a bit of luck to get you into the first team because opportunities to impress are few and far between. The manager didn't go to every reserve game. He would pick a handful out over the season when he could make it and the games fitted in with the first-team schedule. I seemed to always have a good game when he was there, I don't know why. As a young player, if you knew George Graham was in the stand watching, you upped your game a little bit and tried that fraction harder. If you were able to make an impression, whenever anything went wrong in the first team George would know you played well in the reserves and you might be in the back of his mind. If you were playing well in the reserves you more or less knew you were nearly there.

If a couple of players in the first team were playing poorly, you were in pole position to get a chance. Sometimes I would sit in the paddock at first-team games almost targeting the players who might be off form to give me an in. The central midfield was fantastic when I was coming through, with players like Michael Thomas and David Rocastle offering that blend of athletic power and technique.

I made my debut alongside David. He had come through the Arsenal youth system and appreciated how much it meant. He was brilliant for the youngsters. He helped me so much, especially when I was set for my first game. It didn't come at the easiest of venues. Although Arsenal had returned from Anfield with some famous victories under George Graham, and were defending champions at the time, Liverpool still carried the huge reputation of having been the dominant team in English football for years – almost as far back as I could remember.

On 29 January 1992 I made my full debut for Arsenal. It came at the end of a month for the club that you could generously describe as underwhelming. The first team went out of the FA Cup in the third round to Wrexham of the old Division Four, which was a massive humiliation. In the league we hadn't won a game, it was draw after draw. And the goals had dried up. We had only scored once in the five games leading up to that trip to Anfield.

My first start. I was scared. We had all seen over the years how many good sides they had at Liverpool and I remember being nervous going up there. We got to the

45

hotel in time for lunch and then went back to our rooms for a rest. I couldn't sleep. You want to go to sleep but you can't because you're thinking about the game. I was grateful to George. David Hillier, a youth-team product who had been a couple of years ahead of me, was out and I got the nod. The manager picked me for this important, high-profile game and what a place to kick-start my career.

The hardest bit was walking down the steps and you see the famous 'This is Anfield' sign and their players are touching it for luck and you think: oh, God . . . You walk up some stairs and then you are on the pitch and the crowd are singing 'You'll Never Walk Alone'. I've never seen anything like this. The crowd are all swaying, and the Arsenal fans in their corner are trying to make their voices heard. It hits the senses. I went to Carrow Road, but this is like leaping up another 200 levels here.

Now I'm starting the game and I always think in the back of my mind: the first tackle has got to be good, the first pass has got to be good. If you can do that you'll end up okay. Anyway, I think the first tackle was good. The first ball wasn't bad. And then you settle down a little bit and after a while you're just getting into what you've been training for, what you've been taught to do, and you just try and do the job the best you can.

I was marking Jan Mølby in midfield. Danish international, loads of medals, he was a very good player. It was hard to get close to him because he was always one step in front of you, a clever player. You try to close him down and he has already passed the ball on. I was very energetic, the work rate and enthusiasm were there, but my passing was a little bit off at times. As a young kid trying to make an impact you can't help running about like a headless chicken. I was doing all right, David Rocastle, next to me in central midfield, was really helping me out. The game was going quite well, 0–0, everything going to plan, and I thought: well, you're doing all right here. I wasn't too distracted by the noise of the crowd, I was just getting on with the game.

Suddenly it all went wrong for me. There was only a minute to go until half-time, I got dragged back into the box because Ronnie Rosenthal made a run and I was tracking it. I was the nearest man and tried to make the vital challenge. He just toed the ball past me, I lunged at the ball but I brought him down and the crowd boiled up, screaming for a penalty. Mølby stroked it into the top corner. I thought: I'm going to get hammered at half-time . . . It was a long walk back to the dressing room. Tony came up to me and tried to gee me up, telling me not to worry about it.

Heading towards the dressing room, I was worried about what was going to happen, what I would face. We were going well at 0–0. But on my debut I have given a penalty away. I know what George is like, I've seen him have a go at lots of players and I'm thinking: he's going to kill me here. I'd had it before in the youth team as well, so I was ready for it, but it is not exactly something anyone looks forward to. You really don't need it on your debut. But George was as good as gold. All I remember is walking in and him saying, 'Unlucky, son, don't worry about it, keep playing the way you're playing, you're doing really well.'

After that you regain some confidence and I was ready to do my best for the second half. We lost 2–0 in the end but I think George looked at my performance within a bigger picture. He said, 'Look, you've made a couple of bad mistakes but it's your first game. You're going to have some bad moments but it's how you get over them that counts.'

I think all good players have got to learn from their mistakes. It is part of the process of becoming an established professional. Certainly Tony Adams did. You look at his career early, he made so many mistakes but he always seemed to come up the other end and score the equaliser or make a winning tackle to get over the mistake quickly. If you dwell on it you've got no chance. I think George saw that my mistakes didn't faze me. In training the next week I was still keen on the ball. I wanted the ball and I was energetic and running around like normal, so I think he pushed me well into the team and he wanted me in the make-up of the squad.

The other thing that sticks in my mind from when I made my debut was that I seemed to inspire a bit of attention from the Anfield crowd. I had this mass of long, blond, curly hair – when I see pictures now I looked like my mum – and they started giving me some grief. They had a couple of songs. 'One Shirley Temple' and 'Where's Your Caravan?' They thought I looked like a Gypsy! It didn't bother me though. I thought it was quite funny actually. If you can't handle stick, you shouldn't be a foot-baller. I probably thought my hair looked good when I was running around a nightclub but, in fairness, it was an era when a lot of people had longer hair – the likes of Kevin Keegan and Charlie Nicholas set the tone in foot-ball. Looking back, it was a stupid haircut. Maybe I did need the short back and sides that would later become famous . . .

After that Liverpool game George started playing me a bit more regularly. I had a few substitute appearances, and began to feel more part of the scene. I had some good cameos and I got a flavour of the squad. They were taking to me a little bit more once I was training with them every day. I was still a bit nervous around them for the first few months, just trying to settle in until they got used to me. When you move up the ladder quickly you don't want to be cheeky, too full of yourself, but it was special to be in the first team at eighteen years old.

Having made my debut I got a big contract. They suddenly offered me a four-year deal while I was still young to be a pro. My money shot up. I didn't have an agent. I didn't need one. They give you a contract, you go away, your mum and dad would look at it, say, 'Oh, okay, whatever, just sign it,' and that was it.

I just wanted to play for Arsenal, it didn't matter about money. Of course I wanted to earn, but the priority was that I wanted to be an Arsenal player, so whatever contract was put in front of me seemed like a result. There wasn't much in the way of negotiations in those days. I do remember how the wages were staggered over the years of your contract. So it might start at £225 per week, £250 the next year, then £275 and you have your little signing-on fee, about ten grand. But, basically, whatever contract they put in front of you, bang, you signed it.

A four-year contract felt like a long time to be agreeing to, but I viewed it more as the club showing their commitment to me – they said they wanted me, which was a good thing. I was so grateful that George Graham believed in me while I was still a teenager.

It was amazing to see what he could create from a relatively small squad. He didn't buy loads of players, he formed a strong team spirit, and he had outstanding organisational skills. He was a manager who knew what he wanted. He was as hard as nails. We all know about the famous back four, with Lee Dixon, Steve Bould, Tony Adams and Nigel Winterburn, and later Martin Keown came back to the club to add his competitive edge to the mix. The way the defence worked together as a unit, all pushing up together, was trained every day. It was pure hard work. George did wonders for the club getting everybody organised. He was very defensively minded, even for the midfield, in terms of what was required to protect and shield the back four – I took some of that into the Arsène Wenger era.

It wasn't always pretty football but the results were amazing. What he achieved with the squad he had, to win the title twice in three seasons and then go on to have success in the cups, was fantastic. Some players were a little bit scared of George. A bit wary to cross his path. Others didn't care. They got away with it.

George was a disciplinarian. He loved fining me. He was trying to teach me a lesson every time. It happened a lot when I was out with Tony and we got into trouble. But he was very well respected by the players. Paul Merson rates him as the best manager he had because of the way he got the best out the squad he had. He won trophies when some rivals at the time had more talented players.

We had a good mix of players, mind you. Although the defence and midfield were best known for their resilience, we had some very skilful attackers as well, like Anders Limpar, David Rocastle, Paul Merson and Ian Wright. The 1991–92 campaign was the season that Wrighty joined from Crystal Palace and he made an explosive impact, finishing up with the Golden Boot. He was a top man. He was really cracking in the goals and he had an infectious personality and you just wanted to be part of it really.

After my debut in that Liverpool match, funnily enough we didn't lose a league game right up until the end of the season. We hit title-winning form, but too late to make up for a below-par start.

My second start came a few weeks after the game at Anfield, in a match at Wimbledon. George Graham told me I would be playing in an attacking role, just behind Ian Wright, as a sort of number 10. In those days it wasn't illegal to have a bet on yourself, and I was priced at 33/1 to score the first goal. I phoned my brother up.

'Jim, put us a bet on, and you need to come to the game, get yourself down there.'

Jimmy came along with my dad. I scored in the thirty-seventh second of the game. Nigel Winterburn took a free kick, Wrighty was in the clear and crossed for me to beat their keeper. I remember running around in celebration and saying, 'I won £330!' I doubled my wages back then. We won 3–1 and I made my way to the players' lounge after the game to find my family.

'You'll never believe it,' they said. 'We missed the train and were late getting to the ground. When we got in we asked someone the score and they said Arsenal were 2–0 up already. We asked who scored. The young kid Parlour up front.'

And they hadn't had a chance to put a bet on. They were fuming . . .

3

Prawn Crackers

Arsenal made history in my second season. In 1992–93 we reached both domestic cup finals, and both of them were against Sheffield Wednesday, who were an impressive side then (they finished a few positions above us in what was the very first season of the rebranded Premier League). My trips to Wembley taught me some memorable lessons.

I started twenty-three games that season, which was good going and a massive step up after just two starts in the previous campaign. I was gaining some amazing experience. It was a thrill to be involved in the cup runs. The Coca-Cola Cup final came first, in April. Having watched a lot of showpiece Wembley games on TV growing up, actually going there – the twin towers, the big crowd, all the trimmings, the sense of expectancy – with a cup at stake, was incredible.

Wednesday had a really good team. Chris Woods in goal, some serious talent like Chris Waddle and John Sheridan, and dangerous attackers like Mark Bright and David Hirst up front. Blinking hell, they were proper opposition.

The build-up chimed with all those memories I had as a kid. Getting on the coach with the cameras filming everything. I remember the experience of walking out at the old Wembley. In those days, because the tunnel was down one end, you had to walk across the pitch, which was sensational. The flags would be waving with 100,000 people in there, and that was so exciting and also nerve-racking at the same time. By then I was used to playing at some important grounds, but Wembley felt totally different. Just emerging from the tunnel and hearing the atmosphere almost stopped me in my tracks – I'd never heard anything like it. You're in the zone and suddenly you're like 'whoa'. And then you line up and meet the officials and your nerves are really jangling. It's good nerves, if you know what I mean. You want to get out there and you can't wait to hear the whistle because you desperately want to get on with the game. When you are involved, the ninety minutes itself can fly by very quickly.

The American John Harkes put Wednesday ahead early on, but we recovered and Paul Merson was Man of the Match. He scored the equaliser and made the winner for Steve Morrow, who was a pretty unassuming guy who had come through the ranks a little before me but never really became a massive player for Arsenal. The big news to come out of the game concerned him – not so much for the goal but for the aftermath.

It was a great moment when the final whistle blew. Personally speaking, with my family there watching, I was immensely proud. To win that cup, my first trophy, was absolutely brilliant. Moments like that are what you are in football for. Merse did his infamous gesture – pretending to down a few pints. And then all of a sudden – bang! Tony Adams went to pick up Steve Morrow, slipped and ended up dropping him. Steve fell awkwardly and as he landed on the ground he broke his arm badly. I was standing next to him. I was right there and I heard his bone go crack.

The medics rushed on and he needed oxygen, it was a bloody nightmare. Steve has just scored the winning goal at Wembley and now he's going to hospital with a broken arm. He couldn't take part in any of the post-game ceremonies.

I vividly remember walking up the old stairs, shaking hands with the guests of honour and getting my medal.

My first-ever medal. And then picking up the cup feels fantastic. We all felt sorry for Steve but we didn't let it spoil our night out. We went to a restaurant in north London, we drunk into the early hours and had a great party.

A few weeks later we were back at Wembley to meet Sheffield Wednesday again but this time it was the FA Cup final. I was far more nervous for that. I don't know what it was. We were camped up in a hotel for a few days beforehand, the cameras were on us filming our preparations, even while we were playing snooker and trying to relax. It gets to you. Everything was so much more intense, the level of scrutiny cranked up for the big one, it made it difficult to just turn up and play as normal. It was hard to sleep. You just kept thinking: FA Cup final, FA Cup final, FA Cup final . . . Will it be the same as the Coca-Cola Cup?

The occasion is far more prestigious than the League Cup, no doubt. Even that same walk across the pitch felt different. The butterflies were bad. I had a poor game, I don't know why. I didn't do myself justice, I played so much better in the Coca-Cola Cup. I got substituted in the sixty-sixth minute, just after Wednesday had equalised. Wrighty had scored for us but it was quite a cagey game and we drew 1–1 in the end, which meant both teams had to meet yet again for a replay five days later.

I remember thinking how I had to make sure that bad game was a one-off and that I would have to be spot on for the next one. But when the team sheet went up for the replay I wasn't in it. I was dropped. It was absolutely gutting. I wasn't even on the subs' bench. Ian Selley, who was coming through behind me, took that place. I sat there watching the game from the stands with some disbelief. I had been left out of what I was hoping would be a special night for me. Looking back, it was that performance in the first game that prompted George to change it.

The replay had a dramatic climax. It was 1–1 again going into extra time, and as time ticked on penalties seemed inevitable, but in the last moment our big centre-half, Andy Linighan, who had been elbowed and had his nose smashed during the game, popped up with a brave header to win it for us. I found it hard to get so involved in the celebrations. When you don't play on the day you are part of it but not part of it, if that makes any sense. I was so pleased we won, for the whole squad and the club, but it is hard to shake off your personal disappointment about being dropped for such a critical game. You know you didn't play and you weren't on that pitch to really absorb the whole celebration.

For Arsenal it was a great achievement to win the cup double, but for me it was a lesson that brought me back down to earth a little bit. My career had zoomed along an upward curve until that point. I realised then that if you play poorly you are not going to be in the team. After that big realisation, every single game becomes so important. Each and every game, you have to focus and make sure you are ready. You're going to have bad games. But it's the application that needs to be right every time.

I didn't pull George for an explanation. I knew I had not been at the races for the first game and it was obvious that would be the reason. I knew what he would have said. 'Look at your performance in the first game, how can I pick you for the replay?'

I don't know, maybe we had been out a bit too much before the first game and perhaps that's why I played poorly and he was trying to teach me that that wasn't on. Because George was good at that, he would come down like a ton of bricks if you overstepped the mark. He would drop you as easily as clicking his fingers.

Being part of the squad but not selected for the team sheet, either as a starter or a substitute, reminds me of another story. Generally you are still required to travel to games, even though there is next to no chance of playing. Attending games at Highbury was a must, but George also used to take nearly everybody to away games.

A few extras travel along as insurance – in case someone gets injured or falls ill unexpectedly. It was on one of these occasions, at the start of the 1993–94 season, that I found myself at Anfield. When you don't know the ropes too well yet you don't know what to do with yourself if you are not playing on the day. There I was at Anfield, a not insignificant venue for me, not sure where I was supposed to go.

So, 2 October 1994 was my third trip to Anfield for a big league game and the ones before had been memorable all right. First my eventful debut, and the following season I started in a game we won 2–0. I was really pleased with how I played and I made both goals, first using some tenacity to run into their box and cross for Anders Limpar, and later picking out a pass to send Wrighty scurrying in on goal. It had been one of the first live games broadcast by Sky in the opening season of the newly named Premier League and we put on a good show.

It was third time unlucky for me as far as taking part was concerned. Or so I thought. I was still a relatively young kid and George was trying to involve me, teach me what different elements of squad life were like, so I travelled up in the Arsenal party with a few others who weren't playing. I had my suit and tie on. We hung about while those playing went to get changed and prepared in the dressing room. I asked one of the older pros, 'What do you do now? Where do you go?'

Turns out the place to go was upstairs for a few pints. I thought: if that's what you do, I will go by the older pros' example. Off we went, five of us, to the bar. Carlsberg sponsored Liverpool and we began to have a drink, a good laugh with the scousers, ordinary fans who were enjoying themselves before the game. I didn't think anything of it. I was a bit merry and thought we would just go and watch the game in the directors' box as an unused member of the visiting party. I was looking forward to it. All of a sudden the door swings open and in marches our assistant manager, Stewart Houston. He looked straight at me. 'What are you doing?'

'I am having a few pints.'

'The manager is going crazy. Get yourself downstairs now!'

'What do you mean?'

'David Hillier has got injured in the warm-up. You are sub.'

My jaw dropped. I had a pint in my hand. One of the senior pros, who I looked up to, came out with a classic, telling Stewart Houston, 'Let him finish his pint, for fuck's sake!' All the scousers in the bar started laughing. Obviously I didn't finish my pint. I scarpered back down to the dressing room. George Graham's face told me everything I needed to know. He was not happy. I got my kit on and went to sit on the bench, stinking of alcohol. I had drunk four pints at the bar upstairs.

Twenty minutes to go, the manager told me to warm up. As I was doing some stretches along the touchline, a few of the Liverpool subs I knew were ribbing me. 'Were you out last night?'

'No, I have just had four pints upstairs!'

I didn't get on, which was just as well, and afterwards I thought I had got away with it. Back in the dressing room, George started to go around the other players with a few words. Then he turned back to me and announced, 'You were in the bar before the game. Two weeks' wages.' From having four pints, I have been sub, not even played, and got fined two weeks' wages. It wasn't ideal.

As the 1993–94 season progressed it seemed pretty obvious we were not going to be contenders for the title. We were turning into a cup team. The season before when we won the cup double we finished tenth – very mediocre by Arsenal's standards. This season was better, but Manchester United were well out of reach. It was time to focus on another cup – the European Cup Winners' Cup.

I don't know whether it was down to my youth, and George preferring a bit more experience with the different challenge of continental football, but I didn't tend to get picked for those early European games. George used to love pitting his wits against foreign opposition. I think he knew how to handle the league at home, he knew how to get the best out of the English game. But being faced with different tactics and different styles was something that excited him. George was a good tactician. He was excellent at organising a team designed to frustrate the opponent, and then suddenly the chance would present itself to pounce to win 1–0. He did it so many times. He even did it at Highbury, where, being at home, the other team expected us to go forward, but we just defended for our lives, didn't let them play and then all of a sudden from a set piece or a bit of magic we could do the damage. I don't think the Europeans knew how to handle it because they had planned to face more adventurous, free-flowing football.

The chant 'One-nil to the Arsenal' started that season in Europe. That was the scoreline that saw off Torino, Paris Saint-Germain and, most amazingly of all, in the final it was too much for Parma. The final held in Copenhagen was the most one-sided game you could imagine. Parma were brilliant. They had such gifted players: Gianfranco Zola, Tomas Brolin, Tino Asprilla. And we were without our top scorer as Wrighty was suspended. How we won was extraordinary to see really. We had one real chance,

Alan Smith guided one in off the post, and somehow we kept them out the rest of the time.

I didn't play in the final but I have got a medal. I am in all the pictures, in my suit and Arsenal anorak. Copenhagen was a massive party, and that carried on when we got home. We flew straight back from Denmark after the game and Tony and I ended up going to the Crown pub in Billericay. We'd been drinking on the plane, landed at two in the morning, and we knew we could do whatever we wanted then really.

I remember getting off the plane and Tony said, 'Come on, let's go out.' So we ended up in this pub run by our mate Paul Edwards, who had also been to the game. We all more or less got back to Essex at the same time and everyone was elated. One of my mates tried to put my medal in the fruit machine. I'm going, 'What are you doing?' It was madness. There were kids on their way to school the next day walking past seeing me and Tony on our bar stools and it was eight o'clock in the morning.

We went out all afternoon as well, we carried on drinking until the next day and then we just collapsed. It was the first time Arsenal had won a European trophy since 1970, so it was worth celebrating to the full.

The parties were something else after those special games. I mean, you probably wouldn't get away with that now. But we just went for it and a couple of days later we were back in training. Believe it or not, our levels in training never really went down. I was always running around as intensely during any session whether I went out or not.

I didn't really feel the effects of alcohol when I got out on the pitch. I could easily get up in the morning and go down to training and have a good sweat-up and do exactly the same sort of work as if I had been living like an angel. I always managed a good sleep, drank plenty of water, and had no problems getting up at 7.30 a.m. feeling fresh enough for training. I'd think nothing of it, and I suspect most players felt the same way. We had one more game that season, away to Newcastle. We got beat 2–0, but that was not enough to spoil the happy mood from Europe.

That summer I went to America, which was where they held the 1994 World Cup, with Tony for our holidays. Travelling was a new experience for me. As a kid I never went abroad. My first holiday was Tenerife with my mates when we were seventeen. I'd not been abroad until that point, ever. George wanted us to enjoy ourselves during the summer holidays but he did warn us, 'Look, don't go too mad. Come back in decent shape.' Tony and I ate and drank so much in America that when I came back I was a stone and a half overweight. George went mad. He fined me two weeks' wages.

Of course, we had some fun in America. I always remember one morning we woke up with a golf buggy outside our house and looked at each other wondering: how did that get there? We'd somehow driven it home. I fell out of it and cut my leg open. Believe it or not, Gary Lewin, the Arsenal physio, was there as well at the same place.

When we got back to Arsenal George told me I wasn't to do that again, to turn up overweight. 'But isn't that what pre-season is for?' I asked. 'Isn't it about getting fit again?' I was cheeky at times, answering back, but the bottom line with George was – he was always right. It wasn't worth trying it on. I think he found the biggest hill in Hertford-shire that pre-season. Up and down we went, non-stop.

Even though I might have been carrying too much weight I could still run. I was never one of those at the back of the pack. I had the stamina to make sure I was at least halfway, if not towards the front. In pre-season we didn't see a ball for a week. George knew fitness was so important in football. Make sure you're energetic, make sure you can cover people. Pre-season was always so tough with George but that was such a strong foundation for the way he wanted to play and get results.

Winning trophies was a great habit that the team had established under George. There were sacrifices for those successes. Some of the more creative players, the flair players, began to get squeezed out. The likes of Anders Limpar and David Rocastle got sold. That style of player didn't fit under George towards the end of his time. Anders was amazing, one of the best players I've seen. Such quick feet and great close technique on the ball, and such clever imagination, but George wanted more of an efficient side. He prioritised a different ethic: if you lose the ball, you get back into shape, funnel back and make a hard midfield four to protect a solid back four. It was like two brick walls.

If talented players went forward and didn't get back quick enough, leaving a gap, George didn't like that. In training we worked on it again and again. If one moves, another moves across, to protect the foundations. It was all about covering each other. He knew with the players he had he could get results in that way and he certainly did. Even the creative players – and you have to have some creative players – knew they had a bit of work to do to make sure they were defensively switched on when the opponent had the ball. The likes of Wrighty and Merse knew that. But you couldn't have too many of them in the team the way George played. You had to have more hard-working players than luxury players. George wasn't the master of 'One-nil to the Arsenal' for nothing. The current team these days could probably do with a bit more of

It all fell apart. One day it was splashed across the papers that he had been involved in taking bungs for a couple of players. He had signed these two Scandinavians, John Jensen and a defender called Pål Lydersen from Norway, and the reports were saying he had taken over £400,000, sliced off the transfer fees from a Norwegian agent, as part of the deal. As players you try not to get too involved in matters like this, but there was a lot of pressure around. With a big investigation going on over a matter of weeks, Arsenal decided to sack George. It was a massive decision. He had won six trophies in eight seasons and was the best manager the club had seen since Herbert Chapman, who had his bust in the entrance hall to Highbury. George was part of the furniture.

Well, everyone was shocked because it was a huge story and because he had been caught. George was a big figure-head at Arsenal, people did respect him without a doubt. That went for the players and everybody involved in the football club. The day he was fired we played Nottingham Forest at Highbury. What a weird atmosphere. George's picture and notes were still there in the programme and everything, there was no time to change anything. But you are professional footballers, you have to go out and perform, even when there is carnage behind the scenes. We won 1–0 with a goal from Chris Kiwomya but nobody could really focus on what the future was going to hold. It was hard to imagine how George would be replaced.

It was a big hammer blow for some of the players. If you were playing on a regular basis and liked George, you were gutted. For others it might have come as a relief, as not everyone got on with him. Whichever side of the fence you were, though, the same thoughts crossed your mind. Who is going to take over? Will they like me? Will they pick me?

David Dein, Arsenal's vice-chairman and the man who was the most natural link between the players and the board, came to meet the squad. He tried to explain what had happened, why it had happened, and what we would do. Stewart Houston was made caretaker manager until the end of the season. We thought: it can't be Stewart, surely not. I think Stewart really thought he had a pop at becoming permanent manager but that wasn't an option for the lads. We didn't think he stood a chance. We never thought he would be good enough to take such a big position.

It was all a bit chaotic. League form fell apart and we lost six games out of seven. We were sinking down the table at a rate of knots. Imagine – we were not even too far from the relegation zone. The thing that kept us going was Europe. In March we went to Auxerre, an excellent, technical French side at the time, with the tie on a knife edge.

I loved those European trips. The whole experience of playing different opposition in new countries, different mentalities and a way of playing you weren't used to. That game was so important because we needed a release from the pressure we were under at home. They had a midfielder called Corentin Martins, who was superb that night. One of the best I ever played against. Just hitting the ball about like a pinball machine. Auxerre were dominant but then Wrighty scored a cracking goal, and we defended with our lives to win 1–0. George would have loved that one.

Then we played Sampdoria in the semi-finals, a tie full of thrills and twists, and we came through the second leg, which was away from home, in a penalty shoot-out. David Seaman was a hero. On to the final. Real Zaragoza. Oh, we should have won that game. We had so many good chances. It probably summed up how things were not going to plan when Martin Keown and I collided accidentally as we were challenging Gus Poyet for a ball. I was marking Poyet. Martin came from nowhere and butted me in the back of the head. There was blood everywhere. Martin's nose was a mess and he had to go off. I got the back of my head stitched up but played on. I think I played all right in the final, one of my better games. But luck didn't go our way.

It went to extra time and it was almost the reverse of the Andy Linighan Sheffield Wednesday situation. Seconds away from penalties they had a player called Nayim who had a go from miles out. It went in. What a disaster. That was my first defeat in a cup final. I'd always been in joyous and jubilant party atmospheres, but all of a sudden you're involved in one that you lose and I remember the dressing-room area was so quiet, so numbed. Everyone just sat there for half an hour, dazed. No one said anything. It was like a morgue. It showed me the extremes of winning and losing.

Sometimes that helps you, because you learn what to expect when you lose and it teaches you, in the darkest way, that you don't want that experience again at any cost. So it fuels you with a sense that you have to win whatever happens. Although it was hard to take at the time, I think that defeat in 1995 put us in good stead going forward. Tony always used to say you learn more from your defeats than your victories.

It had been a pretty eventful few weeks, and it was about to go into overdrive when we went on a post-season tour in the Far East. The lads were let loose, and without George's influence to make sure we knew there were at least some boundaries, we went crazy for about ten days. We had so much drink, I have never seen anything like it. We played one match and Nigel Winterburn actually tackled me in the game. I said, 'Nigel, you are on my side, remember?'

One day a few of the lads went out and found an Irish bar and we had one drink too many. We were a bit worse for wear by the time we made it back to our hotel. I was rooming with Tony on the tour. We got into our room, and as I was in the bathroom I could hear him on the phone to someone. I thought: what's he doing? By the time I came out the bathroom he was already sparko. About an hour later I had gone to sleep too, but as I am a really light sleeper I woke up suddenly when I heard this knock on the door. I thought it had to be Stewart Houston, having got wind of us being out late. I looked through the peephole to check but it wasn't Stewart. I could see a little man in uniform outside.

'Can I help you?' I asked.

'Room service.'

'No, you must have it wrong, we've not ordered any room service. Must be someone else.'

'Room service for Mr Adams.'

I opened the door and this guy brought in seven trolleys of sandwiches. Tony had somehow ordered thirty rounds of sandwiches. I was parking these trolleys all over the room – one between the beds, one in the bathroom, wherever I could find a space. I was absolutely surrounded by sandwiches. Typically, at 8 o'clock the next morning Tony woke up feeling right as rain. He looked quizzically around the room. 'Were you hungry or what last night, Ray?' he asked.

It was a brilliant trip but it was spoiled on the last night. Naturally we made it a big one. We knew we had to be back at the hotel to get on the bus for the airport at eight o'clock in the morning to go home. It must have been about seven o'clock when we set off from this nightclub, Joe Bananas in Wan Chai, Hong Kong, a popular area with tourists, to find the hotel. I was with Tony and Chris Kiwomya and we were so drunk we had no idea where we were going. We took one pathway and accidentally ended up in the Triad gangster area. It was full of lunatics.

We were starving and had picked up some prawn crackers from a street vendor somewhere along the line. I don't know why this happened and I can't explain why I did it, but as we passed a guy looking under the bonnet of his taxi, I threw a load of these crackers in his bonnet.

This guy hit his head on the bonnet as he looked up to see what or who caused this commotion. We were all falling about laughing, and just carried on walking. The next minute, we've got local people attacking us from all angles. There was another bunch of English guys walking back in the same sort of direction and suddenly everyone was at it. All I did was try to defend myself. Someone went to swing a punch at me and I just hit this guy. Boof!

Tony had run off in one direction, Chris, who had a scrap with someone else, ran off in another, and all of a sudden the police turned up and I was arrested. It was the worst feeling in the world.

I was still drunk but when I got in the police van going back to the police station, it started sinking in. I realised it was eight o'clock, then half past, and that made it worse, knowing everyone was gathering to get the flight home.

In the meantime, Tony had sobered up quickly. Back at the hotel he knocked on the chairman's door. 'Excuse me, Mr Hill-Wood, we've got a big problem. One of the players has been arrested and got into trouble in town.' The team flew back but Paul Johnson, who looked after the players as travel manager, stayed on so I wouldn't be left totally in the lurch with nobody to guide me.

All day I was in prison and one of the guys who had been fighting Chris was in the same cell as me. So I jokingly said, 'All right, mate? Yeah, I don't like Chris Kiwomya either!' Chris was a great bloke, but I tried to lighten the mood a bit and, besides, I didn't want another punch-up. We had to try to keep our spirits up. We sobered up in that cell and the more serious thoughts began to sink in. I didn't know what was going to happen. When you are in another country it is even more alarming. You are fearful of what scenarios might come up.

That evening they let me out on bail. I went back to the hotel. It was just Paul Johnson and me left from the Arsenal party in Hong Kong.

'Shall we have a couple of beers, Paul?'

'What? You're joking. We're supposed to be going back to England with the team now, but look at us.' The barrister the club had called for me, Adrian Huggins, came to meet us that night. He told me that I was facing a serious offence in Hong Kong. 'You'll probably be lucky,' he said. 'You might get away with six months in prison.' Six months, just for having a silly fight. I could not believe what was happening. 'I'll do my best for you,' he said on his way out.

That night I didn't sleep one wink. Six months in a place you don't know, it's going to be disastrous. Next morning I put my Arsenal suit on and we went to the courthouse – there were dozens of cameras outside. Obviously it was big news that an Arsenal player had been arrested. I remember walking in and sitting down. The barrister stood up and confirmed my name, mentioned Arsenal Football Club and apologised to the taxi driver and the people of Hong Kong on my behalf for everything I had done. He didn't say a huge amount in my defence. The judge announced my punishment was a fine of 4,000 Hong Kong dollars – the equivalent of £180 – and some compensation of around £100 for the man I hit. So I ended up looking at

Before I was a Gunner. My first club was Fulham. Before that I played with my brothers and for my Sunday team.

At the age of fourteen, Arsenal signed me as an apprentice. From day one, I learned what it meant to be an Arsenal player. I knew it was my club.

Aged sixteen, we were at Arsenal every day. It was dog-eat-dog. We had the likes of Andy Cole and Paul Dickov keeping me on my toes.

My first team debut was in 1992 but I had a Weston Super! Gave a penalty away at Anfield.

I was soon up and scoring… but the crowd gave me a bit of stick for my hair. 'One Shirley Temple'!

Had the privilege to meet this man on tour in South Africa when I was twenty. I wanted to take him down the pub but I reckon he was too busy at the time.

As a young player, Tony helped me massively. I looked up to him as a kid of seventeen, eighteen. He was my role model. He was the one who took me under his wing.

From the training ground to playing with Wrighty, I always enjoyed spending time with everyone at the club.

no more than £300, when I had been worried about a six-month jail term. It was nothing. I left court with the photographers snapping and couldn't wait to go home.

We headed for the airport. Paul was going back then with or without me, but thankfully I was free to get back to England. I had the cheek to ask Paul if he wanted a few beers on the plane. 'No, bloody not!' he replied.

As we got off at Heathrow there were even more cameras. Walking through the airport with my Arsenal suit on, in disgrace, it wasn't good news. The headlines back in England did not make pretty reading. 'Arsenal Ace Nicked in Red Light Punch-Up' was all over the *Sun*. 'Parlour Has Shamed the Nation' wrote the *Mirror*. That summed up the take on what I had done. One of the papers ran an interview with the chairman, Peter Hill-Wood, which emphasised how badly it all went down. 'Football and Arsenal need this like a hole in the head,' he had said. 'When will footballers learn? He has let down not only his team-mates and the club but England as a nation. It was foolish behaviour.' I remember thinking: I can't do this any more. I can't. I have to knuckle down.

I had a meeting with Ken Friar, Arsenal's managing director and a man so steeped in the club he had been there for decades. Ken asked me to go and sit down with him at Highbury for a chat. I was still a young lad really,

I was still learning, twenty-two years old. Tony came back with me to the ground because he wasn't driving and I was giving him a lift, so I left him in the Bank of Friendship, a pub which is just down the road from the marble halls of Highbury, while I went to face the music.

'Mr Friar, before you start, I am really sorry. I know I put Arsenal's name in a terrible light and that we got bad publicity.'

'Absolutely,' he replied.

'Look, I'm really sorry, that's all I can say.'

'Well, I'm fining you two weeks' wages.'

'I totally accept that. It won't happen again.'

'Yes, you had better make sure it does not happen again.'

Two weeks' wages was what I expected so I took it on the chin and was about to head out the door to go to pick up Tony. I was ready for a pint with him. As I was walking out, Mr Friar stopped me. 'Ray, come back a minute, we've got another problem.'

'What's that?'

'The barrister. We have his bill here. Obviously Arsenal got the best lawyer they could find in Hong Kong.'

'Yes, Mr Friar, thanks very much for getting me that.'

'We arranged it, but you have to pay for it.'

I looked at the bill. It came to £12,000. 'Mr Friar, I am only on £400 a week. How am I supposed to pay £12,000?'

'Well, you are due a £15,000 signing-on fee in January so we can take the £12,000 out of that.'

What could I say? I couldn't believe it. All the barrister had said was my name and that I was really sorry to everybody and wouldn't do it again. Twelve grand for that. Incredible. I got to the Bank of Friendship and explained it all to Tony over a much-needed drink. 'Twelve thousand pounds? And two weeks' wages? I'm paying Arsenal to play at the moment. I would have done six months for that!'

Many years later, at the 2015 FA Cup final, I bumped into Ken Friar and we ended up looking back at that incident. 'I was only teaching you a lesson,' he said. 'In that case,' I replied, 'I have learned it by now. Can I have my £12,000 back then?'

With hindsight, the whole episode was absolutely terrifying. My parents were not happy but they knew I got up to silly things and maybe hoped this would show me that ultimately I had to be responsible for my actions. My girlfriend at the time was pregnant with my first kid as well. I didn't even phone her from Hong Kong to explain what was going on, so I basically left her to see the news for herself. You realise how much awful publicity something like that brings and how it affects your reputation and the amount of trust people have in you. The Hong Kong debacle made me grow up quickly. I had to learn some lessons sooner or later.

4

Crossroads

Arsenal needed new guidance, a new direction. Little did we players know at the time that, during that summer, David Dein mentioned the name of this guy he knew, Arsène Wenger, to the board, but they were not too keen on something so unfamiliar, a gamble, when we needed clear leadership. English football had more or less always relied on British management at that point.

Of course we talked about it a bit. Who would it be? Everybody knew the size of Arsenal Football Club: we needed a big name with enough authority. It's all a bit unpredictable. We all knew what it's like when a new manager comes in. You are on trial again, simple as that. Nobody is guaranteed their place. Maybe the older pros felt more confident on that front, but the youngsters certainly didn't. I was one of those thinking: who will be next? Will they like me? Will I be involved?

Arsenal went for Bruce Rioch. He was a Scot with a reputation for liking discipline, so I suppose the idea was for someone who followed on in the George Graham mould. Under the headline 'Rioch's Regime', one of the stories in the papers gave a strong impression of what we could expect: 'Short hair, don't be late, wear a tie, be polite, and get married.' I didn't know him personally, but I knew he'd done a good job at Bolton. You have to give people a chance and I felt like I got on all right with him in those early training sessions. He seemed to like me, he put me central midfield and he wanted me to be an important part of things. He encouraged me to stay behind after training and practise with him. I really liked him. He gave me a new contract, which I was very pleased to sign.

He thought he could do well but, looking back on it, it was just too big a job for him. There was one mistake he made. He kept talking about Bolton. All the time he would tell us about Bolton and their players and what it was like there. We were all thinking: what? Look, you are at Arsenal now. This is jumping up several levels. No disrespect to Bolton but Arsenal is bigger in every way. At Bolton he could control everybody but here he had walked into a dressing room with some imposing characters with huge experience behind them, and the more he kept banging on about Bolton, the more the players were getting fed up with it.

Bolton was a smaller place. He could probably keep on top of what the players were doing and where they were going. But at Arsenal in 1995 the Tuesday Club was going strong, everyone was having a good time, and I don't think Bruce could handle it at all.

Then he fell out with Ian Wright. Wrighty was bigger than the manager at the time. You can't fall out with your top striker, the man who was idolised by the crowd and got on well with everyone at Arsenal, from the tea lady to the directors. Bruce wasn't having it with Wrighty from day one. There comes a point in the dressing room when the rest of the players are looking at this situation – a problem between the manager and the best striker – and you know it's going to be costly.

Wrighty was very important to us. He's a free spirit though. I think Bruce wanted him to work harder up front. Bruce was always honest, he could be blunt, thinking it would provoke a reaction. He didn't mind conflict. But Wrighty didn't respond well to that sort of thing. He needed a bit of leeway and George used to give him that.

George knew how to handle Wrighty very well. He got the best out of him by letting him get away with a little bit more than the others. But he did that confident that, come Saturday, which is what it's all about, Arsenal would be scoring goals and getting the best out of their main man. Wrighty was the one who would get into the areas where he knew the ball was coming and put it away: simple. But Bruce couldn't let him and his own spark be.

It was difficult. You've got to respect the manager. I respected him, but if half the players aren't having him, then he's got no chance. Unless everyone pulls in the same direction, wants to be together, you won't win nothing. Everything got on top of the manager in the end and he didn't know what to do to try to rein everyone in.

Into this environment walked Dennis Bergkamp. Arguably the best signing that Arsenal ever made. Dennis is an absolute legend and a brilliant player. Instantly you could tell how amazing he was. He was an absolute dream for a striker – if you score goals, you want someone like Dennis behind you, teeing you up with great chances thanks to his magical technique and vision.

It was Arsenal's good luck that he was finding it hard at Inter Milan – Dennis was a quiet man who just wanted to do his football, come away from the football environment, and then have a normal life. In Italy you can't do that. People would follow him around and he found that unnerving. I don't think he really settled in Italy, so Arsenal made their move, and what a fantastic move it was. It created huge excitement. The fans were elated to find out Dennis Bergkamp was signing for Arsenal Football Club, it was a massive thing.

The Dutch mentality and the English mentality are quite similar. He loved it straight away. He was very quiet, as you'd expect, and we were always very chirpy and rowdy. But the mix worked. Straight away we were so happy to have Dennis around and he was happy to be around us. Dennis loved the team spirit, the bonding and camaraderie that was part of our group, eating our lunch together and having a laugh around the place. People don't see that side of him but he was a very funny man day to day, one of the characters who kept the dressing room upbeat.

He was the one that changed our whole attitude towards training. Just watching the way he handled himself from day one was an eye-opener. It made you think: hold on a second, I need to up my efforts here. He was so professional: the way he trained, the way he conducted himself every day. Some players could train really poorly and play really well come Saturday. Later, people like Patrick Vieira and Marc Overmars went through the motions sometimes in training but, come kick-off, they were unbelievable. It was like Patrick's brother turned up to training while Patrick himself would be the one strutting his stuff Saturdays. Other players could train really well during the week and have a nightmare Saturday. Arsène bought a player called Alberto Méndez, who was amazing during the week but couldn't handle the crowd in games and looked useless. Then you had the type who would have to train hard all week to play hard – I was one of those players. I couldn't go through the motions and suddenly turn it on come matchday.

Dennis was similar in a way, as if he knew he needed to keep himself finely tuned all the time. Even when he arrived, well into his mid-twenties and an established star, he was intent on improving his technique by staying behind after training, chipping balls onto the bar on his own. Again, again, again. You're thinking: he's a much better player than us and he's practising more? He wants to keep that level or even raise it. That changed our attitude. I started to stay behind after training then and work on my game a little bit more.

At the same time that Dennis arrived, David Platt also came from Serie A. It gave an impression that Arsenal were changing in outlook. David was a good lad and he had learned a lot of good habits when he was out in Italy. He used to talk about what he experienced abroad and he also had a great career for England. David didn't play all that often once Vieira and Petit became established but he was an ideal person to have in the dressing room at a time when a lot was going on. That summer when Dennis and Platty came was a sign of changing ambitions. Arsenal were trying to be something a bit different.

We didn't have a great season in 1995–96, we were too inconsistent. We went on a bad run as the campaign was coming to an end and needed a win in the final game to qualify for Europe with a spot in the UEFA Cup. Our opponents that day were Bruce's old favourites, Bolton, and we won thanks to a thunderous goal from Dennis.

I think some of the more senior players went to see David Dein, perhaps expressed a few concerns. It wasn't a complete shock to me when Arsenal decided to get rid of Bruce, although the timing was dodgy – just one week before our first game of the new season. It was a bit unfair, he had not even been there for a year.

With football changing quite rapidly at the time – continental stars joining and all the new glitz from Sky TV and more money pouring into the Premier League – Arsenal wanted something more forward-thinking. Bruce was old school. Arsenal wanted to move in a more modern way. The main objective was to try to win the league but, even though finishing fifth that season was a step in the right direction, we were nowhere near challenging for the top. The board chose to make a bold decision. It is not very nice when someone loses their job and I felt bad for Bruce, but it turned out to be one of the most pivotal moments in Arsenal's history.

Here we were again, for the third time in a little over eighteen months since George's departure, wondering who and what was around the corner. We started the 1996–97 season without a permanent appointment. Stewart Houston was drafted back in briefly and then my old youth-team boss, Pat Rice, stepped in to hold the fort as a temporary manager. There was a load of pressure on the board as they were tight-lipped about what they were going to do. To not even have a proper manager for the first few games didn't look good.

Three days before the first game, at home to West Ham, Arsenal signed these two blokes from France. We didn't know anything about them. One was a midfielder who had played a handful of games for his country, Rémi Garde, and the other was a tall kid from AC Milan called Patrick Vieira.

Things were moving at quite a pace. When I first got into the team in 1992 the team was overwhelmingly British. There weren't many foreign influences around. Maybe a couple at most top-division sides. Everyone more or less felt like they were in the same boat. With more players coming from abroad, we all started to try to get used to each other's ways. And there was an awful lot to learn.

People like Dennis Bergkamp and Patrick Vieira were certainly not familiar with the drinking culture that had been a part of our footballing lives for so long. I cannot imagine that they would have ever seen the kind of behaviour that was second nature to us.

There was a period where Tony and I used to go to the pub every Sunday. It was usually a rest day, as invariably we played Saturday, so the following day we were free. Every Sunday we would meet at the Chequers at noon. We were a group of seven lads, Tony and me and our local mates. If you were late there was a £50 fine, a bit like George Graham, straight into the whip. I used to make sure I missed the traffic, got there for 11.50 a.m., and would stand outside the pub with ten minutes to spare until opening time.

Amongst the seven of us we had to agree a time to go home, and nobody could go home early. 'What time today, lads?' We went round the room saying our times – 7 p.m., 3 p.m., 7 p.m. . . . . We took a vote and the majority won. If it was 7 p.m., you couldn't leave before then, otherwise it would be a £200 fine. Tony's rules. No problem. The guy who put forward 3 p.m. basically had to stay until 7 p.m. Usually we had around ten pints.

One week we all arrived on time, high noon, same old crowd. What time today, lads? Tony said he had to go at 3 p.m. in the afternoon. We all looked shocked.

'Are you feeling all right, Tony?'

'Lads, I have to.'

'You can't! The rules are the rules. You made them up. If anyone else wants to leave early, they can't.'

'Nope, I've got to go.'

We didn't think much of it. A few pints later, it's almost 3 p.m. and a car pulls up outside the Chequers for Tony Adams. The driver comes in to collect him. Tony is hammered. We asked him where he had to go that was so important to muck our game up.

'I've got to go to do the FA Cup draw live on television.'

We were astonished. This car had been sent from FA headquarters in Lancaster Gate to pick him up for the draw. We couldn't wait to watch it. We sat round the TV in the pub, and there was Graham Kelly, the FA chief executive, introducing proceedings. 'Welcome to the FA Cup draw, and picking the balls we have two special guests today, the England manager and captain . . .'

The cameras panned to Terry Venables, who looked immaculate in his suit and tie, hair neatly combed. Then the camera pointed to Tony and he was swaying – shirt hanging out, trainers, a right scruff. The camera pulled off him straight away.

When it was his turn to choose a ball, he put his hand in the pot, his hand was swirling around. You could see Terry

Venables thinking: take a ball, Tony. He pulled the ball out and said 'Thirty-one'. The problem was, thirty-one wasn't in the draw. He was told to have a closer look at the ball – it was thirteen. In the end they had someone behind him checking that he had said the correct number of the ball he picked out. We were in stitches in the pub.

By the time it got to 7 p.m., everyone was getting ready to go home, all of a sudden the same FA car pulls up and Tony gets out. 'Did I get away with that, lads?' he asked. We had to tell him it was one of the funniest things we had ever seen. He produced the £200 fine for leaving early and announced the new leaving time was 1 a.m. We ended up recreating the draw in the pub in fits of laughter.

Fast-forward. September 1996. London Colney. The Arsenal squad were all at the training ground and Tony called a team meeting. Personally speaking, we had roomed together for years, become firm friends, we went out and got involved in all sorts of shenanigans, but I had no idea what he was about to say. He gathered all the players together and told us he was an alcoholic.

A few of us were just looking at each other, not sure what was going on. Blimey, I thought, some of us drink more than you, Tone. It was a sense of incomprehension really. If he was an alcoholic, perhaps that meant we must be alcoholics as well. What is an alcoholic? I don't know. Is it waking up in the morning and needing to have a beer? I always thought Tony was more of a binge drinker to be honest. It was more that he would go out and carry on going out for a couple of days, but he could be off the booze fifteen days and it wouldn't affect him. I don't know what kind of stage he was at. All I did know was that it was an incredibly brave thing to do.

The thing about Tony is that he had so much willpower and, once he made a decision, he'd always go with it. I think it was affecting his life. He wasn't happy. He loved socialising, he loved going out, but he just wasn't happy. There was a feeling of despair. None of us can know for certain how others are feeling deep inside.

I think Euro 96 did him in. Tony was captain of his country for a tournament on home soil and England had a really good competition. After all the build-up, going out in the semi-finals to Germany, on penalties, hit him hard. On top of that I think he had his off-field problems with his wife at the time. He was wondering if he was being a responsible dad to his kids. People think that footballers – especially ones who are leaders like Tony – can handle anything. But real life can get very complicated and then how good you might be at your job doesn't come into it.

Tony said to me, 'Ray, I really enjoy going out with you, but if you're going out don't phone me up.' So I said, 'Of course not, Tone. I respect what you're doing and I really want to help you, all of us want to help you as much as we can.' I'd still go out and have a few drinks with my mates but we knew Tony wouldn't be coming. He was very strong and we all respected how he was trying to live his life.

I'd still go to training with him every morning. I still was his room partner for every away game. Nothing changed there. We'd go to bed earlier on the Friday night before the game. Nine o'clock we might be closing the curtains. And then it would turn out Tony would be up all night watching telly and it would be me nodding off early in bed if I was catching up after the odd night out.

Having said that, I slowed down. The Tuesday Club faded out. Tony giving up drinking was one of the best things that ever happened to me. I was easily led. My career was at a crossroads at the time. Was there a danger I was going to throw it all away? I was definitely at the point where it could go either way. It gets to a stage when you are twenty-three and you can't be called a youngster any more. Which path are you going to take? This way or that way? You either pick the road where you really want to make it and stay at the top. Or you don't. I didn't really fulfil my potential as a youngster and that was down to me.

I still went out but nowhere near as much. I made sure I only went out at the right times, which was the biggest advantage. Obviously after games we'd go out and have a drink, or on a Sunday with a day off. I stopped drinking during the week when we were training.

The timing was perfect for me with the huge broadening of our horizons and knowledge. Attitudes changed a lot. Everybody realised the game was becoming much more professional. The message was obvious: if you want to stay at this club then you have to make the change. I did, for the better. I felt like I had been gifted another chance to make the best shot at my career.

What a stage of my life to meet Arsène Wenger. Most of us were not sure how to react initially to Arsenal's new manager. When he first turned up, a few weeks into the 1996–97 season, nobody knew him or what he was going to do to the club. We just had to trust him. We just had to trust the word of David Dein, who told us all, 'This man will take us forward. He is going to transform the club.'

I was asking Tony Adams, David Seaman, everyone. Who is he? No one knew. Even the new French lads, Rémi Garde and Patrick Vieira, didn't know him very well. In English football you were used to at least getting a manager that you knew something about, usually whoever comes in has been around the block a few times, you have an inkling about their character. There were some suggestions coming in that this Arsène Wenger was going to be really strict. I thought: oh no, am I going to fit in with this regime?

Luckily, those suggestions were well wide of the mark. When we first met him he didn't look or sound like any manager we had ever known. The first day at London Colney he came out looking more like a teacher than a football man, and he got us all together and spoke really well. He had a big focus on pushing the club in a progressive way. He told us he was going to give everyone a chance to stay with the club and be part of it. He wasn't one for making big demands and rushing into decisions. 'I'm going to watch the training for the next few weeks and I'm going to be honest with you guys and say who I want and who I don't,' he said.

So we were all on trial. He knew all about the famous back four and how solid they were and he had plans for them already. The training was so good. I became so switched on. I am not saying I didn't enjoy it under George Graham, but when Arsène Wenger came it was suddenly much more stimulating. Technically I realised where I had to improve to become a better player. I did work hard. Arsène would be the first to say that. I really wanted to be involved in this team. With the likes of Bergkamp, Ian

Wright, Tony Adams, Patrick Vieira, there was the nucleus of a great side.

The first few training sessions are always vital for a new manager. If the lads enjoy it and start to feel he has new ideas, and gives the impression he knows exactly what direction he wants the club to go, then everybody signs up to it. The training methods were fantastic and I couldn't wait to go in every day. It was always different, always made your mind work.

This man was perfect for me to improve technically. He made us think about the way you pass the ball. We improved our awareness of what was around us. We played a lot of small-sided games and for that you have to know where everybody is and how they are moving. You develop a picture in your head of where your next pass is going to go.

It's not rocket science, but if you pass the ball in front of someone so they can take possession of it in their stride, it's much more efficient than passing to where they're standing, where they have to take a touch before they start running with the ball. Then everything is faster and sharper. I used to stay behind after training sometimes, maybe to work on my left foot or my general play. If you ping a pass 20 yards to a specific spot several times in a row, how many times will you get it right? If you get nine out of ten right you know you are improving.

Arsène was always there to help you as well. He never said, 'I've got to go now.' You could stay out as long as you liked and he would be there to give you a helping hand. He is still like that now, when I go up to visit London Colney I see him out there in the middle of the training sessions.

I really put my head down. The way I had been before was the product of the environment I was brought up in. I loved going out with the lads. But things were changing straight away. Dennis had already started that change. For such a special talent to be practising like you can never believe was an eye-opener. We realised that we had to practise more, we had to put our hours in, to make sure the consequences came out on a Saturday. That is when it really kicked in that it was time to knuckle down. I knew I had ability but the concentration and application were what required hard work. Maybe if I had learned that lesson earlier I might have made more appearances for Arsenal. I didn't because of all the drinking and socialising.

If I was at a crossroads when Arsène arrived, then the timing was perfect to ensure I went in the right direction. It was a time where a lot of things came together. The influence of the manager, new continental players arriving, Tony stopping drinking, not going out so much.

Arsène's ways helped me to change as a footballer and a person. He is a very genuine man. He didn't want to hold anyone back. Go out and play. You had to be organised and know what you were doing, but he did want you to express yourself, without worrying about mistakes. Arsène was more open-minded than George. He stressed how he wanted us to be positive and trust our own ability.

Training was always sharp. What he did really well, Arsène, was change the timings of how we organised sessions so everything was really sharp. No disrespect to any other manager, but Arsène knew exactly what the time span was to keep everything fresh. As soon as you were losing it, he was clever enough to set up another drill that was totally different to reactivate your mind. We all looked at each other thinking: this is something else. It was enjoyable.

He created a perfect balance at training to ensure we stayed focused and fit. It was an art form, never too much that you overdid something or got bored. It was fifteen-minute bursts, which worked just right. Players lose their concentration easily otherwise. Doing the same thing for twenty-five minutes doesn't necessarily do you more good. The focus was on high-quality work. If the quality was there in that fifteen minutes, that was enough. It was time to move on to the next exercise. The next thing was normally something totally different to what you had just done, which keeps your mind working, your motivation high, and everything fresh.

Some would stay behind for stretching and massage and so on. The most important thing for a footballer is recovering for the next game. As you get older that is the hardest bit, too. When you are in your early twenties your body is still young and you can get over it quickly. Once you get to your late twenties and thirties that's when you really need to stretch. This new approach was why a lot of the older lads were able to prolong their careers. The famous defence – Tony Adams, Steve Bould, Martin Keown, Lee Dixon and Nigel Winterburn – was proof of that. They started stretching out, Arsenal had this guy, Philippe Boixel, coming in who was unbelievable. For forty-five minutes he would push your body all over the place, he knew all the important pressure points, nobody had ever seen anything like him, but it felt great afterwards. You felt energised. Afterwards, you'd go and see him once or twice a week and he'd put your knee over here, put your fingers in your mouth. If you had any slight pains or anything, you'd tell him and he'd push something here or there and by the next day you were good as gold. It was a masterstroke from Arsène.

There was a big incentive to reassess the way we were looking after ourselves. Eating healthily, stretching routines, vitamin supplements. There was a bit of a fuss about this stuff called creatine, which was supposed to give you strength and energy. I just took anything. Whatever was in front of me. I knew he would never give me anything illegal. I just thought: it can't be harming you, so if there are big caffeine tablets or there's creatine in bowls, in we go. Whether it helped you, even a little bit, I don't know.

It has been well documented that Arsène introduced a lot of changes about diet and how we were refuelling. I was one of the biggest eaters anyway. I would make sure I ate a lot. I didn't mind vegetables and all that, so I liked it. I didn't eat chocolate anyway, but Nigel and some of the others wanted their treats. They'd still get chocolate and put it in their bag. Those guys were thirty years old. It's harder to change your habits when you're that age.

But we were coming out of a different era. We had an eating competition once on the way back from Newcastle. It was a six-hour journey so we were like, 'What should we do today? Let's have an eating contest.' No reason really, it was just something to do. We must have had about eight dinners. Bouldy won by a mile, he had nine. In the end we had to stop, a few of the players were being sick outside the coach. But under Arsène those days were becoming history.

We were encouraged to always drink water, which I did anyway. I didn't like orange juice, and a lot of the lads had lemonade. It was either beer or water for me. I remember Arsène stopped the drinking, which was part of respecting Tony as well. There was no more alcohol in the players' lounge on matchdays. Some of the lads were moaning. Sometimes you have to relax after a game and a drink can help to slow down the adrenalin. Also it was about trying to offer a good time to our guests. What about our families, who might want a drink? But if that's what the manager wants, that's what happens. So that was stopped.

The toning down of the drinking culture came from a combination of both Tony's situation and Arsène's philosophy. It affected our socialising to an extent. But you could feel that it was the way football needed to go anyway in terms of professionalism and looking after your body better. When Arsène came in, that really improved. By that stage it was obvious the old attitude wasn't good enough. Football was changing, more foreign players were coming into different teams, and the whole scene was being transformed. You had to be more on the ball. Because if you are marking someone who's not got up to what you've got up to all week, they are going to make a fool out of you.

Looking back at it, it was a big adjustment to all of the habits we had grown up with. Once we started winning games and being successful everybody truly bought in to Arsène Wenger's ideas. We all want success. If this man can show you how to win trophies, he is worth following.

So much about our daily football life felt different to how it had been under George. Arsène wasn't even much of a disciplinarian. It really wasn't his thing. He did have rules around the place. When you come in from outside you take your shoes off at the front door. No phones. But those sorts of things were being regularly broken and it got to a point he tried to give us a talking-to.

A mobile phone went off while he was trying to tell us off. Then, not long after, about four mobile phones went off all at the same time and that was it – he'd had enough. 'Right, that's it! No more phones! The next phone that goes off, there will be a £10,000 fine.' And he was serious. So everyone turned off their phones, pronto.

A couple of days later we were at a hotel. Our routine was always the same: go for a walk, come back for our little stretching routine of twenty minutes, then we would go for lunch. The stretching was always very quiet. You couldn't hear anyone talking, no chatting, it was just a time for relaxing and almost meditating.

All of a sudden, a phone goes off. This is two days after the threat of a £10,000 fine. It kept ringing and ringing. All the lads started panicking. 'Whose phone is that?' snapped

5

Inspector Clouseau

Arsène Wenger liked our pre-season training to be concentrated, somewhere peaceful, and the perfect environment to get set for the intensity ahead. We went to Switzerland for his first pre-season, in the summer of 1997. During that close season we bought a group of new players and they were integrating into our squad – the likes of Manu Petit, Marc Overmars, Gilles Grimandi – as well as a younger group of prospects like goalkeeper Alex Manninger, Matthew Upson in defence and Luís Boa Morte in attack. We already had good players and in came some more, so there was no reason to think we wouldn't have a real chance this season.

As the tour was winding up, come the end two weeks of really hard, committed training – we didn't even see a drink – we had a team meeting. We were going home the next day. Arsène spoke to us. 'Lads, you have been superb,' he said. 'You have done everything I asked you to do. You deserve to go out tonight.'

For the English boys, that was the sign to go down the pub. The French lads were heading to the coffee shop. Gilles Grimandi was a great lad, a funny man, and he wanted to get into the English spirit. He came over to me and asked, 'Ray, do you mind if I come out with you lot tonight? I don't know what you guys get up to but I would like to see.'

'Gilles, come out with us tonight,' I said. 'You will have a much better time.'

So we all met in the hotel reception, about 6.30 in the evening. We walked down the road about 100 yards and we were in this pub. There were only five of us, and I will never forget, one of the boys went to the bar and said, 'Thirty-five pints, please.' We turned to Gilles. 'Do you want a drink, Gilles?'

'A small glass of wine, please.'

So there were thirty-five pints of beer lined up, and a small glass of wine at the end for Gilles on the bar. He looked around. 'Who else is coming?'

'Nobody, Gilles. This is our starter.' We had seven pints each ready to go.

His face was amazing. 'How can you run around and play football?'

We had a good laugh and ended up really slaughtered because we hadn't touched a drink for a couple of weeks. Later on that evening, we were walking down the road and the French lads were sitting outside a café, all smoking. Being the cheeky chappy, I couldn't resist. 'Lads, how the hell are we going to win the league this year? They are all smoking and we are all drunk!' Gilles was laughing away. He loved the atmosphere. He explained that in France it is totally different. It's a job, they all come in, do their work, and don't necessarily speak to each other. They would go and train, have a shower and then that's it, go home. So we were trying to get it across to the French lads that we're all mates, we can all have a laugh.

Manu Petit didn't get it to start with. I'm sure it was just that he wasn't used to it rather than arrogance, but when we would come in we would say, 'Morning' and not get much of a response. Once he had more or less ignored a lot of the lads, we told him we might want to cut his ponytail off if he kept blanking people. After that he was good as gold. 'Good mornings' all round to everyone every day! He just didn't realise the mentality, that was all, and at the start did things as he was used to doing back in France. He was a tremendous player who, once he got going, was an integral part of the way our team functioned.

The mixing of two quite different approaches turned out to be one of the keys to the team's success. The English lads realised how hard we had to work on our technique and how to look after ourselves better. The continental lads learned to love that little bit of fun. When we train we train hard. You only train for an hour and a half so you concentrate, you focus on your position, you've got to see what the other players in the team are doing. So that was always really intense, good-quality work.

But it's that bit before and after training. In the changing room, or in between drills when we had breaks, we'd have a laugh and muck about. Arsène Wenger really loved it as well, because he had not been used to that mentality as a manager with his work previously in France and Japan. He had a great sense of humour about it. He loved having all the banter with the lads, he recognises you can't always be serious. It's impossible. You've got to have some light-heartedness as well, making people more relaxed, especially if you've got new signings coming in. The atmosphere was like being on a footballing version of a building site.

You could see the new boys sense: oh, this is a good place to be. We always made them feel at home, whoever it was, we always tried to make them feel part of the team. Even if some of them were a little bit surprised at how relaxed we were and how much we messed about, they got into that. But, crucially, when we got on that training field we knew exactly what our jobs in the side demanded of us, and exactly what we had to do.

Marc Overmars made a big impact straight away. He was a funny little character. Like his fellow Dutchman Dennis, it was easy for him to fit in. Marc was the one who gave me my nickname. We were in training one day and I went around two or three players, nutmegged Dennis, smashed the ball and it went right in the top corner. David Seaman did not move. Little Overmars ran past me and said to me, 'You are like the Romford Pelé.'

My reaction was, 'You don't even know where Romford is, do you?' And he said, 'No. Someone told me you come from Romford.'

That afternoon we had a press conference and it was his turn to do it. The line of questioning was all about whether we could beat Manchester United to the title; they were the ones to finish ahead of. The press were full of it, testing us out to see if we could pose the threat.

Little Overmars came out with this: 'Yes, we definitely win the league because we've got the Romford Pelé in our side!' That ended up in the papers, and it seemed to stick.

Everyone started calling me Romford Pelé, which was quite embarrassing at the time.

It was just a brilliant dressing room and everyone learned to love it. Even someone like Dennis, who people might not have expected to get too into the banter – he rarely went for a night out – had a brilliant dry sense of humour in our group. He would always wind up Martin Keown. Martin would kick Dennis in training, but Dennis was forever getting him back with his jokes.

Dennis was great. He really got into the spirit of things. We went through a stage where we were pulling people's shorts down at silly moments. And if Dennis could get someone when they least expected it, he couldn't resist it. He got me once when I was about to go on as sub in a pre-season game. There was a big crowd behind me and he pulled my shorts down! I pulled them up lightning fast.

Once at the training ground, Dennis got our kitman Vic Akers big time. All these women came up to London Colney from L'Oréal, they were giving packs out for people's wives, girlfriends and whatever. A few of the staff downstairs got wind of it and wanted to go and see what kind of freebies were on offer.

Vic arrived and put his arm up against the wall, leaning there trying to look all cool and casual, and said, 'All right, girls, what have you got?' As the girls were trying to explain, Dennis in the meantime crept up behind him and whipped Vic's shorts down. His shorts were around his ankles and the women looked completely shocked, didn't know where to look. By the time Vic pulled his shorts up in embarrassment we were all on the floor crying with laughter. It was one of the funniest things I've ever seen.

You had to watch Dennis. In the end you had to tie your shorts up quite tight to guard against it. I was involved in it too but it was just a bit of fun. I was probably the worst culprit for mucking about. Some of the French boys wondered how I got away with it half the time. How are you going to win the league like that? In my opinion it's crucial to have friendship and good times amongst the group. If on the pitch you are in trouble, your teammate is not going to help you if he doesn't like you. You've all got to get on.

A few of us liked to go and play golf. One time there was a big golf day that Ian Poulter had organised – it was before he really cracked it on the professional golf circuit – and we had a nice four made up of Dennis, Alex Manninger, myself and Vic Akers. We turned up and a lot of Arsenal fans were there, and Dennis was a bit nervous, believe it or not. He had just started playing. He was a decent standard, round about a 24 handicap, and he was improving but he could be erratic. Off the tee he could scuff it, that kind of thing.

There were around 300 people watching round the first tee. I could tell he was thinking: I'm not liking this. He thought he was just coming down to play a game of golf and then go home. I said, 'Dennis, it's all right. All you have to do is make sure the first shot you hit is a good one off the tee, down the fairway and that's it, done.' He hit a corking shot. All of us cracked one straight down the fairway, we picked up our bags and off we went. As we set off, Dennis was talking about how nerve-racking that was.

We walked 50 yards and realised the crowd was all following us. Dennis said, 'What are they all doing?' They followed us, all standing round the green watching us putt, then on to the second hole. I parred the first hole and everyone was clapping. Because Dennis was such a good footballer there was a perception he would be confident and good in everything he did. He was cacking himself, which we all thought was funny.

The second hole I hit one that nearly killed someone. This crowd was lining up as if they were watching pros, thinking we were good players. Unsurprisingly, after that a few started drifting away. We were hitting balls all over the place. By the sixth hole there were probably only three people still left watching us. It was an enjoyable day, if a little bizarre.

Tony was changing his lifestyle in a big way but it wasn't like he was suddenly on the edges of the dressing-room banter. When he gave up drinking he found new hobbies. He was telling me about literature, coming into training with really long words, sounding very clever. I said, 'That's brilliant, Tone.' One night he told me he had started to play the piano. I thought that was fantastic. I'd love to play the piano. He said he was six weeks into learning a song, and if we give it another fourteen or fifteen weeks he would perform the song for me.

I didn't think much more of it. One day we were playing away up north, the same crowd at the back of the coach – Bouldy, Nigel and Lee Dixon – when Tony pulled up in his car and got his things out the boot to load onto the coach. He had a portable piano of some kind. 'Look, lads, he's got his organ with him!' We would sometimes tease him about getting him back on the booze – the lads could drive you mad like that – and it was a gift to see him with this organ.

He has now been learning for twenty weeks and gets on the coach to tell me he is ready to play the song he has been practising for me. After dinner, a lot of us played cards. This one night, Tony came along and told me to finish up by 9 p.m. so I could hear his song. He went back to the room to get set up. I remember looking at my watch at 8.50 p.m. and thinking: I've got to go, no more cards, it's time for Tony's song. I had a really good hand but I was out.

Tony had set his organ up, he was testing his synthesiser, making sure he had the right amount of bass. I went quiet with anticipation and there it was . . . 'She'll be coming round the mountain when she comes'. I was gobsmacked. Twenty weeks for 'Coming Round the Mountain'? I was expecting Bach!

The next morning at breakfast the lads were desperate to know what the song had been. There had been sweep-stakes, all sorts of bets. I gave everyone a guess, and if any-one got it I would give them £5,000 of my own money. When I told them, everyone was flabbergasted, saying, 'That's it, it's time to get him back on the booze.' We were only mucking about of course. We would never do such a thing. If he had ever come out with us and wanted a drink we wouldn't have let him have it. We all had such respect for what he had done and his courage in dealing with it. The first few years were difficult for him. But once he had got over that phase he would come out with us and just drink water. Some twenty years with no drink-ing is an incredible achievement. That must be so hard to do, especially in a pressurised environment like football. If I don't drink for a few days, after a while I just fancy a beer with my mates.

Around 1997–98 a lot was changing off the pitch in the background. When Arsène came in the amount of staff grew quite quickly, so there were a lot of new faces around and it was important that they became part of our daily life as well. New staff were joining in all departments. Sean O'Connor came in to run the training ground, we had new masseurs and fitness experts. Then the Arsenal chef turned up. I don't think when most of these people arrived they knew what a football team was like, the way the characters were and how we behaved. Rob the Chef tried to get in with the lads really quickly. Every time anyone had a birthday he would make a big cream cake for them. We would come up at lunchtime, there would be a rendition of 'Happy Birthday', blow the candles out, and Rob presented this cake for pudding.

One time it was Lee Dixon's birthday and Rob made a massive cream cake to celebrate. We decided to test Rob out. Let's sniff the cream. We were all sniffing at the cake and making faces. 'This is off,' I shouted. 'We can't eat this. I don't think the chef is any good. He's useless.' Rob came marching over. 'What do you mean?'

'Smell that, it's not right.'

At the time Rob didn't know the kind of guys we were, and how the camaraderie worked. As he went to smell his creation we couldn't resist the old pie-in-the-face routine. He had these big glasses on and all the cream was stuck round his glasses. The cream was in his beard. We were all laughing and he joined in. That was the turning point for him. If he had got the hump we would have got him every week. But because he laughed he was accepted. After that he became one of the lads.

That day Arsène Wenger came in late for his lunch and the chef still had all this cream around his eyes and his beard. Arsène looked at him. 'What have you been doing?' When the chef explained the lads had thrown a cake in his face, Arsène laughed. That was the sort of episode the manager, and the foreign players, hadn't really experienced on the Continent but they thought it was brilliant. They had never seen anything like it before. It was a big part of what made being at Arsenal special for them.

It is important to have good people around the team behind the scenes who are a big part of your everyday life. That's what keeps the team going sometimes. At Highbury there was an Irishman called Paddy Galligan who looked after the ground, he even lived there. He had this flat that was part of the West Stand. He was always hanging about on the stairs outside the marble halls and was a big character. In George Graham's era we used to go with him to the Bank of Friendship pub. Paddy was the main man for loving Arsenal Football Club. He used to come into the dressing room after games and have playful mock fights with people and all sorts. The players would wind him up and he would end up growling away. The role people like Paddy can play should never be underestimated.

Getting ready for our first full campaign under Arsène, we felt good. Arsène always wanted you to have a really good holiday and come back feeling refreshed. Pre-season was different to what we had been used to. We didn't see a ball for a week with George. But straight away the balls are out on the first day, nice and easy. With other managers it's up the hill – the biggest hill they can find. So the training methods were completely different, which was the first sign of the plan going forward.

Arsène broke it down to three blocks; everything prepared, down to the finest detail and divided to the tiniest measurement. The first block we're going to train hard but not too hard, get your legs back into moving. After five weeks off, I don't think it works going back into running really hard as you might pull your hamstring or your calf. Arsène always had quick groups and then he had a slower group, so you didn't feel the pressure to keep up with the others, you could go at your own pace. That block would get harder as it went on.

The second block would be pushing it; you'd be going up to the next level as you're back into the mode of playing football, although mindful of your fitness – you don't want to overdo it and get injured. Then it gets tougher as you go on tour. That's ten days away and you train really hard twice a day. Lots of games. That's when you're really peaking and should be getting up to the kind of levels you should be at.

The third block, the week before the opening day of the season, you go back into the mode of how you live and work around matchdays. You play, you recover, you train and get your tactics ready, and then by Saturday you're as fit as a fiddle, ready to go. It is all planned so that you should feel absolutely ready for that first match of the season. Some other clubs had a fitness test on day one of pre-season. What's the point of that? It's not about being fit the first day of pre-season, it's about the last day.

It's the biggest buzz you ever get, running out into a big stadium to that packed crowd, playing the game and winning. That is what you prepare all week for. That's the manager's job, to get us into the best condition possible for that moment, to prepare us for crossing that white line.

The manager can't change it once you've crossed that line. Yes, he can make substitutions, but he is really at the mercy of how his players play on the day. People say it's a manager's job on a Saturday but I don't believe that. It's a manager's job Monday to Friday to make sure you're fully prepared, know what you're doing, for the weekend game. If you're a player, your responsibility is to not let yourself or your mates down.

Arsène likes to create the right structure and atmosphere, but let players take some responsibility. You still had to do your job in certain areas of the pitch, and then in the final third you could express yourself, go and take people on. We did a lot of pattern-play work. We practised our movement – it wasn't luck. We got off well that season and were unbeaten from the start in the Premier League for almost three months to set us up nicely.

We grew into a super team. We didn't have a big squad but those who played regularly handled their roles confidently and those who came in when we had any injuries or needed to make a change did a fantastic job. We had David Seaman in goal, the famous back four along with Martin Keown, and sometimes Gilles Grimandi, taking care of defence. In midfield Patrick Vieira and Emmanuel Petit were sensational together, with myself and David Platt in there as well. Once we got the ball we could look up to find Dennis Bergkamp or Ian Wright. This new kid Nicolas Anelka came in and caused havoc for the opposition defence, and Marc Overmars was destroying people from the left-hand side.

The jigsaw just fitted together with that team. You have to have the different pieces, a bit of everything. You have to have workers, you have to have clever, technical players who can unlock the door, you have to have defenders who can't stand conceding a goal, and scorers who live for that feeling of the ball hitting the net. You need the blend though. The team doesn't function without it. When our puzzle was complete it was an outstanding team to play in. We all valued what everybody brought to the party.

I think the formation in midfield was crucial for us. Everyone said we were 4-4-2 but really it was more fluid than that, as quite often it turned into more of a three up front. Marc Overmars was playing on the left wing and he scored sixteen goals for us that season. When he went rampaging forward I dropped in to help the midfield. It was something we did automatically.

I had it drummed into me under George Graham that I should tuck in to bolster the midfield. So when we had Overmars playing unbelievably on that left-hand side, and at times he was our main threat, we would all shift over. Manu Petit would go across to fill in for him when he was on the attack. Then Patrick would shift over and I would fill in for him. So we could have three strong players in midfield while we let Overmars dart forward and get back into position when he needed to. Once we won the ball back I'd go out wide again on the right. And it worked. It was instinctive more than anything else. It was probably down to George Graham and me knowing how to shuffle across, while Petit had been a defender so he knew what he was doing to provide cover.

We lost our first league game on 1 November. Derby away. Trounced 3–0. It was the start of a slump that saw us get beat in four out of six games. During the season you get ups and downs, which is why it was so extraordinary to go unbeaten some years later. It was usually November for us when we'd have a bad spell. I don't know why. We started so well in the league, but by November maybe we got a bit tired. Arsène couldn't work out why we would do so badly in November. But it was like we would drop a level, and then have to pick it back up again.

This particular nasty November tipped into December, and the last game of the blip was all over the press as a proper crisis moment, as we got beat 3–1 at home to Blackburn. Marc Overmars put us in front but we fell apart in the second half. I remember the game really well. When Kevin Gallacher scored to put them ahead it was a bad moment, and there was a lot of negativity around at the end of the match. A few harsh words were exchanged. Tony was struggling with his fitness and after a discussion with the boss he had a break, which enabled him to come back stronger. That's typical Arsène.

What Arsène does that is totally different to George or anyone else is that he never says anything after a game. A lot of managers like to have their say straight away in the dressing room. Arsène never said anything after the game. He always liked to look back on the video a couple of times and have the meeting on Monday. He never really went into anyone, he wasn't that sort of character anyway. Other managers I'd worked for would lay into you immediately, blame you, before even watching the video back. He was very calm, even when Arsenal played poorly.

That Monday meeting was so important though. He wanted feedback off us as to why we felt we hadn't done so well. After everyone had had their say he would tell us, 'You know how it went wrong, so let's avoid it happening again.' In that meeting there were a few home truths and it had so much good impact in terms of the team bouncing back. We knew we had a winning formula in our squad. We were very focused on recovering some form.

Our next game was Wimbledon away, three days before Christmas. It was at Selhurst Park, which they were renting at the time. A few seconds after the second half started, with the game still at 0–0 but us looking the better side, the lights went out. Floodlight failure apparently. There was an announcement that they would have to wait twenty minutes to try the lights again in case they blew a fuse so we went back to the dressing room.

Now for a little background. At this point I have to explain that I used to call Arsène Wenger Inspector Clouseau. He could be a walking disaster. He'd fall over the nets, get tangled up, couldn't get the balls out. I used to love Peter Sellers, I used to watch all the Pink Panther films when I was younger and Clouseau was my favourite character. Arsène Wenger shared some of those foibles, so I couldn't resist choosing that nickname.

We used to bring all the Pink Panther box sets and videos with us when we were on the coach to games. The English lads at the back are laughing and all the French lads are like 'What is this?' But Arsène would be laughing too, he used to love it. It so happened that on the way to Selhurst Park we were watching the one where, with his infamous accent, Clouseau describes a bomb as a 'beum'.

At Selhurst Park, Arsène was late out of the dressing room at half-time, he'd gone to the toilet, so we went out to play and before you knew it the lights were gone and we came back into the dressing room. I sat down next to

Tony Adams and Arsène comes out of the toilet to see us all sitting there. 'What is this?' he says. 'What is going on?'

In my best Inspector Clouseau accent I said, 'There's a beum in the stand.' I thought he didn't hear me. Tony looked at me and whispered, 'You idiot. What did you say that for?'

Arsène looked round. 'What did you say, Ray?'

I just had to make something up. 'We should be winning this game,' I blurted out.

We went back out for a warm-up in the dark as they were going to try putting the lights back on, but they failed again immediately. The game was off. A few minutes later they flashed a message on the scoreboard: 'Merry Christmas . . . Anyone got any 50ps?' The game ended up being rescheduled.

We finally managed to get that Blackburn defeat out of our system on Boxing Day, beating Leicester at Highbury. We were off on a new run. It might not have been the best game ever but all good runs have to start somewhere. Turned out we didn't lose a match until May, when we had already won the title.

We had some unsung heroes in that fantastic run, a few players who stepped up to the plate when we really needed them. That is one of Arsène's greatest skills. He always made the players around the team feel wanted. Even those who were not playing every week felt certain they had a major part to play in the season. There is a real art to doing that. If you are not playing on a regular basis, how do you keep those players involved and ready in case they are needed? Arsène worked wonders in that department.

When we replayed that game at Wimbledon the man who came in and scored the crucial match-winner was Christopher Wreh, a striker from Liberia who wasn't a first choice. Wrighty was out for a while and to take the pressure of Anelka, who was only a teenager, Wenger was giving both Christopher and Nicolas games.

A couple of weeks later we had a tough game at Bolton away. No Bergkamp or Wright. Wreh found the winner again there, and also in the FA Cup semi-final against Wolves. These were key games and the deciding goal came from a bit-part player. But he knew he was a vitally important member of the squad, for we needed him to come in when injuries took hold. We also had Alex Manninger play some huge games in the run-in as David Seaman was out for a few weeks. He was fantastic, and kept a load of clean sheets. Alex was intensely competitive, always highly strung. He used to play golf with Vic Akers, the kit man, and me, and he was so determined. There was one time he put the ball down and hit it 30 yards into the woods. He said, 'I will find that ball,' and I said, 'Alex, no you won't.' He was in there fifteen minutes looking for his ball and came out with a load that weren't his. So he goes back to the tee, hits the same shot and straight back into the woods again. 'I will find that one.' Here he goes again, marching off to the woods. By now there are ten people waiting behind us and they're getting the right hump. Alex didn't like losing. In fairness to him, he was unbeatable in those games he played in 1998.

Another youngster, Luís Boa Morte, came in and did his bit during that period. He scored a penalty in a shoot-out at West Ham to keep us in the FA Cup that season. We were up against it, Bergkamp had been sent off quite early in the game, but these young players were all trusted by the experienced players to do the business. And they did. They all played a massive part that season.

How do you keep everyone together as a unit? That is the hardest thing for any manager. Squads were smaller then, so it was a little bit easier to instil that real team ethic than today, when there are twenty-five players expecting to play every week. The spirit of togetherness that Arsène harnessed in 1997–98 was probably what won us that double.

Manchester United had won the title for the past two seasons and were favourites again. They were so good. This was the first time in a while that we had been able to take on their midfield. Looking back, that section of their team had real quality. They had Ryan Giggs in his prime, David Beckham on the right, and Roy Keane and Paul Scholes. That was the area of their team we were always worried about.

They were top of the league for weeks. But we started stringing together win after win, and feeling stronger and stronger. It all came to a head when we travelled to Old Trafford in March. Crunch time. They were actually nine points ahead of us but we had three games in hand.

What Marc Overmars did that day was incredible – I've never seen a right-back get ripped apart like that. The kid's name was John Curtis, a big prospect at Old Trafford. He got taken off at half-time, it was embarrassing. I felt sorry for him in the end. Overmars was quick, technically smart and was having a brilliant season. He was scoring goals, making goals, and was a nightmare for opponents. You've got to have an outlet of pace, and the combination of Marc and Nicolas Anelka gave us two really exciting options.

It was a massive game; I remember the winning goal vividly. When Anelka flicked it on, Overmars ran through and he finished it off so coolly. I can still picture how it felt just standing there and looking round. I remember having the feeling right there and then that we were going to win the league. Going to Old Trafford to get that result felt so significant. A draw would have been good enough for Man United at the time to keep it in their hands; it might have stopped us in our tracks a little bit. Certainly that bus journey on the way home was lively. The bus was always buzzing after you'd won a game anyway, but this was extra lively. We thought that might be the nail in the coffin for them. We can go on and win this.

We still had some challenges up north, but we'd reached a point as a team where we felt we would win every game. We went to Bolton and they put us under a lot of pressure – really we never should have won that game. A few of the Man United players were in the stand, they had come to watch. They worried we were catching them, and that's the kind of place you can lose points easily. But the thing about our side was that we could really stand up for ourselves. If they kicked us, we'd kick them back. We had enough players able to mix it, especially the back four, if it got a bit nasty. We had both sides in our group, the substance and the style. We beat Bolton 1–0.

I loved it when it got feisty. There's a passion that sparks up. On the whole there were a lot of fair tackles, real hard honest tackles. Not just from us but from other players as well. When it got tense, you could sense the atmosphere in the crowd crackling. The fact we had the appetite to mix it was a good thing for the club. We knew we had great players who, when we had the ball, could play as beautifully as anyone. But we could also put a tackle in. We could look after ourselves. Arsenal probably don't have as much of that nowadays.

We went to Blackburn in April, the team that had taken us to our lowest point at Highbury in December, and took them apart. I scored two goals, and we were lethal on the day, 3–0 up in the first fourteen minutes. We ended up winning 4–1, and the confidence we all had was sky high. We were closing in on Man United and they knew it. Our next game we smashed Wimbledon 5–0 and finally went top of the league. Psychologically that was important – that position we had been chasing for a while was ours and we knew we had to keep playing well to keep it.

Momentum was with us and we won ten games in a row to confirm our status as Premier League champions. That honour came at Highbury, with a 4–0 victory over Everton. That game produced the fondest memory of my footballing life, when Tony scored that last goal. I know what Tony's like – that ball could have gone anywhere, in the stands, top tier, against the bar, anywhere. The way it happened was perfect, with Steve Bould producing the assist by chipping it through to his fellow centre-half. Tony chested it and smashed it on the half-volley, a difficult skill, straight into the net. That was an awesome moment, and now a statue of it is outside the Emirates Stadium. I remember celebrating with Tony and it meant so much.

We still had a couple of league games to go, and then the FA Cup final against Newcastle. Still, that night we went out. We went to Dover Street wine bar. I remember Matthew Upson trying to outdrink some of the more experienced drinkers and he ended up – how shall I put it? – 'losing'. The kid was only nineteen. It wasn't the wisest move to try and take on the big boys in a drinking competition. Matthew didn't stand a chance, but I suppose being part of a squad that wins the league at that age, it feels like you can achieve anything.

That year was amazing. It was my first title. For me, titles are very special. You go through the highs and the lows of the season, see who's most consistent and, when it really matters, who can handle the pressure. When you're in a cup competition you're just playing the game and you either get through or you don't. When you're in the league though, when you get close, you have that week waiting for the next game so the pressure builds. Don't get me wrong, when you get to the semi-final in the cup there is real pressure. But as you get closer to a league title there is a nervousness – good nerves, exciting nerves – but you still have to manage that situation. Once I got on the pitch

I was fine. The pressure? I enjoyed it. Some players like it, some don't. We used to rise up to it. It didn't always go our way but a lot of the time during that era it did. I felt very lucky that we had a lot more ups than downs.

The FA Cup final against Newcastle was something I was particularly looking forward to, as I wanted to make sure I had a better experience personally than back in 1993. There was a disappointment for us when Dennis Bergkamp missed out with injury. Newcastle, our opponents at Wembley, had a decent side then. Stuart Pearce was marking me, Alan Shearer was up front, so we couldn't take anything for granted.

I remember it was really hot that day, boiling hot. We had to be on the ball but we got the early goal. It was that man Overmars again, with a burst of pace, to dink us in front. They hit the woodwork a couple of times in the second half, before Nicolas Anelka sealed it. He was on fire at the time. I hooked the ball over the top for him, and once he was racing towards goal he was ruthless.

He was a quality player. He didn't smile a lot. When he did smile, we started rubbing him on the back, saying he had wind. We were only mucking about though. It wasn't easy for these guys, it would be like me going to France when I was nineteen, that would be terrible. I wouldn't know whether I was coming or going, so credit to him.

Obviously it was so important to have the French guys around. Rémi Garde didn't play that often but he was a lovely bloke, Gilles Grimandi was a great lad. Emmanuel Petit and Patrick helped Nicolas. If there hadn't been any other French guys I don't think he would have come over. Luckily for us he did, in an amazing piece of business by Arsène Wenger.

I ended up getting Man of the Match in the FA Cup final, which was a really proud moment. All of my family were there to see it. By 1998 I had ensured I'd improved, worked on my technique, compared to the player I was in 1993. Arsène was always very fair. He'd say to me, 'Play well and you play next week.' And as a player that's all you want to hear. I think he knew when I went out there I would give 100 per cent, and that I was improving as a player. It was a brilliant season, I did really work hard I must admit.

At the end of the season, Dennis Roach, an agent who knew Arsène fairly well, organised a tour for us. We had a lot of fun. For some reason Marc Overmars brought along a fart machine. He was letting this thing off even while Arsène was doing a team talk.

How Dennis Roach put up with us I will never know. At one point we had a boat trip. It was very upmarket, with some local dignitaries in the Far East. Dennis Roach was sitting next to one the most important people, a lady, and he was trying to give her all the charm. Overmars put the fart machine into his jacket pocket. As he's eating his dinner, all you can hear are fart noises, the woman didn't know what to do. Then Dennis went off to the toilet, passing by us all, saying how wonderful the food was, and while he was away from the table we put half a bottle of Tabasco over his dinner. So he came back from the toilet, started eating and he had to eat the lot as he'd said the food was so fantastic. He was sweating.

On the last day Dennis Roach told us, 'Lads, you've been great. Thanks for coming. All the drinks are on me tonight.' Tony Adams went to bed but some of the rest of us went for it. The best whisky, the finest champagne, we were buying everyone in the bar drinks and we were giving tips – three months' wages worth of tips to the waiters for bringing the drinks over. Tony had a counsellor that used to travel with us, Steve Jacobs, and he made the mistake of giving one of his keys to us before he went to get some kip, saying we could use his room instead of waking our own roommates up.

After another drink or two we decided to get him. One of us had the idea to set his quilt alight. He went crazy – 'Get off, you prats!' – but we put it out pretty quickly. Then a bit later I went down to reception and told them the man in Jacobs's room was poorly with sunstroke and we needed a doctor as quick as possible. Because we were in the Arsenal party they jumped to it.

I'm waiting outside the room. Steve Jacobs has a quilt round him. Next minute the doctor comes up and I said, 'Look, doctor, he doesn't like people touching him, he hates it, you might have to dive on him.' We stood in the corner and the doctor is going one way and Jacobs is going the other. The doctor actually dives on him, they're rolling around on the floor.

When I got back to my room, Tony gave me this lecture. I had a quick shower, got my tracksuit on and headed to the bus. Jacobs was on at us, telling us we were crazy. The next minute Dennis Roach comes down. I shouted out, 'Watch this, lads!' He went to reception and asked for the bill. His face changed completely. Then he got on the coach and said, 'You had a nice night last night, didn't you, lads?' We thanked him for his hospitality. In fairness, he paid it all without any complaints, not that he had too much choice.

6

Short Back and Sides

After such a fantastic end to the season my hopes were up that I might have a chance of going to the 1998 World Cup that summer in France. In my youth I won a few caps with the Under-21s. We had done well. With a team including Sol Campbell, Jamie Redknapp and Robbie Fowler, we went to the Toulon Tournament in 1994. We had a right good laugh.

We were down the beach most days, we'd have a couple of beers – we forgot where we were really. We would get back late, 8 p.m. instead of 7 p.m. There was a goalkeeper called Alan Nicholls, who sadly ended up dying in a motorbike accident, but I do remember one time he had twelve cigarettes in his mouth and lit every one of them up for a bet. Just as he did it, the door opened. Ray Wilkins was one of the coaches and he wasn't impressed. 'You are with England, son. What are you doing?' It was a bit all over the place but we won the tournament, beating Portugal in the final, so something was going right.

I was Man of the Match in the final, and came back and flew straight off on holiday to Ayia Napa with my mates. That was during my crazy period. We were lucky in those days that people didn't have mobile phones to snap footage of what we got up to, like today's young players have to watch out for.

I won one England B cap, but graduating to the senior team was a gradual process for me. During Glenn Hoddle's era I got called into a few squads, without actually getting into the team or on the bench. Glenn was a very good coach on the pitch. He got the job when he was only thirty-eight and could still play with such finesse. The sessions were always lively.

Just getting in the squad was brilliant, going away with the lads. I knew a lot of them from the Under-21s, and obviously was friendly with some of the senior pros like Tony Adams. Gazza was always great fun, a bit of a lunatic but so good to be around. Man United had their own table, they got there early and had a spot near the balcony, because they had so many players in the squad – all the rest of us were mixed up.

I was hoping for a chance in the first team, especially when I was really enjoying my football and doing well in the season leading up to the 1998 World Cup, but David Beckham was in front of me. The problem I had is that once you play on the right-hand side of midfield, which I did then, then that is your position. I could play centre midfield as well, where obviously you have two slots, so more chance of getting into the side. If the guy on the right is fit and playing well and he is David Beckham, you have no chance of getting in the team. The manager is not going to put you in centre midfield for the sake of it if that is not where you play week in week out for your club. My options were limited.

Even so, by the time the 1998 World Cup was coming round, the papers were really pushing my case to be included in the England squad. I could not have been playing any better for Arsenal. Impossible. We had won the double and I had played my part in that, and was thrilled to have won the Arsenal Supporters Club Player of the Season award when we had a squad with the likes of Dennis Bergkamp, Patrick Vieira and Marc Overmars in it.

But an infamous story caused major problems for me when it came to Hoddle's England. As we were getting closer to the tournament Glenn told me I would be in the team for a friendly. The trouble was, I arrived for England duty carrying an injury. I had tweaked my calf in training that week with Arsenal. Gary Lewin, who was our club physio and also worked for England, knew exactly what I was like. I played through so many injuries if I could. So I went to see Gary to ask for some advice. 'Gal,' I said, 'my calf is really sore, can you have a look at it?'

He said it was a bit tight and asked how I felt when I was running. The truth was, when I pushed off it was catching. He reckoned I had probably pulled a few fibres. I was gutted. I was supposed to be playing that weekend for England and, as a player, there are not many prouder moments than that. I was so disappointed, as I knew how well I had been playing for Arsenal and was raring to take my opportunity. If you lose your place you may never get it back.

I had been told I was going to be playing in the game. I was about to go for a scan to see how bad it was when Glenn Hoddle came in and asked, 'What have you done, son?'

'I think I have pulled my calf slightly. I am about to go for my scan but I'll be so disappointed if there is a problem. I can't believe it.'

'Well, before you go for your scan I want you to go to see Eileen Drewery, my faith healer.'

'Who is that?' I had never heard of her. Little Robbie Fowler was next to me and he started laughing.

Gary Lewin jumped in. 'Okay, Boss, I will send Ray straight up.' When Glenn left the room I said, 'Who the hell is that?' He told me to just go up and see this lady the boss was recommending.

So I head up to her room, knock on the door, walk in and there is this chair in the middle of the room. She told me to sit down. I sat down. She closes the curtains and I think: oh, is this a strip joint? Is Eileen about to take her clothes off? It was bizarre. Next minute she's walking round me, then she goes in the bathroom, and I'm thinking: what next? I can't work it out. I've got a bad calf. So now she's circling me and she puts her hand on the back of my head – I had long hair back then – and I just said, 'Short back and sides, please, Eileen.'

She starts laughing, I start laughing, I didn't think nothing more of it. I went for my scan and was due to be out for two weeks. Later on, Eileen told her husband she thought it was funny. He was at the bar, as he always came in for a few pints, so he then told the players and everyone was laughing about it. But someone told outside the group and there it was on the back pages of the tabloids. It got out of hand because the papers really wanted this Eileen Drewery. So I made a splash in the newspapers, a mocked-up picture of her with her hands on my head, which I'm not very proud of.

When I got back to Arsenal I was playing really well. The next England squad comes out and I'm not in it. Dennis Bergkamp was like, 'What is going on?' I said, 'I don't know, I think it's something I said . . .' In hindsight, it might have made life easier if I really had gone out and got a short back and sides years before when I got stick from the crowd for my long hair.

Arsène Wenger had been Hoddle's manager when they were together at Monaco and as Arsène had noticed how I had been pushed to the side, he said he would try to find out what was going on with Glenn. I remember Arsène coming back to me and saying that I wouldn't be playing for England again, not under Glenn Hoddle – I had disrespected his faith or some such thing. When we see each other now Glenn says he doesn't remember that, but that was the message that came from Arsène.

So now we come to the main training camp ahead of the World Cup selection, where thirty players travel but some will be let down in order to trim the squad to twenty-two. England went to La Manga, where an episode blew up because Gazza smashed the room up when he didn't make the squad. I was never even invited to La Manga, even though the media were making a big case for me to be involved. I had already given up on that happening.

That summer I was distraught. Everything on the TV was the World Cup. The papers were full of the World Cup. I'd just won the double, I should be on that plane. So that summer I got married instead, which cost me a fortune.

Seeing Glenn now, he's good as gold. But he went through that period when it was difficult for the players to totally grasp what he was about. If Eileen Drewery could get me fit when I was injured, then she'd be worth multi-millions of pounds. That's just the way he was. I did actually get into one more squad that Glenn picked, the first qualification game for the Euros that followed France '98, but I didn't make it into the selection for the match.

Then he got sacked for making ridiculous comments about disabled people. Kevin Keegan came in and the England scene was totally different. He was a lovely man, a great laugh, although tactically we were never going to win anything with him. He was more about fun, I felt like it was going to Las Vegas with him for the week. It was all gambling, card schools, sports, race nights and everything was going on.

I remember one evening a couple of days before a match we were expecting to watch a video of the opposition after dinner. But Kevin stood up and told us all the evening's viewing would be a race night. We used to take it in turns to be bookmaker, and this time when Kevin asked for volunteers. Alan Shearer and Teddy Sheringham put their hands up. 'We'll be bookies, Boss.'

What we didn't know was that Kevin had already watched a video of the races and knew the results. Then he rewound the tape and put it back, ready to start. We all went back to our rooms for a bit before the race night began. I got a knock on the door. It was Kevin. 'Back number six in the first race,' he said. He went from room to room, telling more or less everyone except for Alan Shearer and Teddy Sheringham.

Once we got started all the money was piling on for number six. Alan and Teddy thought we were just guessing. The video is playing, and the commentator was saying, 'Number six will struggle to get a place today . . .' Alan and Teddy looked pretty pleased. As the race started number six was right at the back. But then as soon as it went around the bend it started flying. Kevin was running round the room hitting his backside with a stick like a jockey. When number six came in first we were all jumping about. Alan and Teddy went white. They had lost a fortune. Thousands of pounds. They couldn't believe it. And there were still another seven races to go. At the end of the night Kevin stood up. 'Great night, lads,' he said. 'The plan for tomorrow is breakfast at eight o'clock, then we will have a little look at *the Racing Post . . .*' As everyone started leaving the video room he called us back. 'One more thing. Alan, Teddy, we have had you right over tonight.' Kevin came clean about number six and that it was all a wind-up. Although Alan and Teddy said they would still pay everybody out they didn't need to. But as a team bonding exercise, it was fantastic. We were all still laughing about it the next day. When you are cooped up in a hotel there are only certain things you can do, so a fun night was perfect to get the team spirit together.

Kevin was a guy who enjoyed having a laugh with the lads. He was a players' manager. I remember one occasion that sums up Kevin and how the players enjoyed his style. We were doing a drill, just to have some fun before the proper warm-up starts, where we were in a circle and if you got nutmegged, you had to stand there and endure another one. We were all having some fun, and someone nutmegged Martin Keown. The next moment the ball is played to Tim Sherwood – and it wasn't him who nutmegged Martin by the way – and Martin launches a two-footed challenge and Tim Sherwood has to be stretchered off. When the teams were picked for a five-a-side after that, Kevin Keegan smiled and said, 'I'm on Martin's team.'

Martin was one of those players who, if you were at war, you'd want him in the trenches next to you, he never gave up, he was hard as nails. He was one of the best markers I've ever seen: seriously, you tell Martin to mark someone and he'll do it, with pace, passion, everything. He really cared about how he was doing. Once he got in a confrontation with a journalist who had been giving him five out of ten in the paper every week. Martin always looked at his score and complained that five out of ten was a joke. We told him not to worry about it, the manager, the players and the crowd know what he's like and that's what matters. Who's bothered as long as the manager picks you next week? He was like, 'I am. I am bothered.'

We played Roma once and Martin's job was to stop Francesco Totti. So Martin was elbowing him, kicking him – Totti lost it and elbowed him back, and in the end they both got sent off.

Later I said, 'Martin, what a great job!'

'Lads, I got sent off though.'

'Yes, but so did Totti and he's a much better player than you, so you did the team a favour!' Martin was easy to wind up and I think he knew I did it with affection. He knew I was cheeky.

England was a really great atmosphere under Kevin Keegan. He gave me my first senior cap in a European qualifier at Wembley, against Poland. I got the experience of playing against Scotland, Argentina and Brazil. I came off the bench for his last game, too, which was the final-ever match at the old Wembley before they closed it for rebuilding, to turn the historic place with the twin towers into the modern arena with its arch. By then results weren't going so well. But, even so, nobody expected what happened that night.

It was a weird scenario. We lost to Germany in the pouring rain. Dietmar Hamann scored a long-range goal. At the end of the game I remember Kevin walking into the dressing room and turning to his right-hand man, Arthur Cox, and saying, 'That's it.' He more or less resigned on the spot. Tony Adams said, 'Don't you want to think about it, Boss? You know, sleep on it and see how you feel tomorrow morning?'

'No.'

Then Arthur Cox tried. 'Wait a minute. Just think about it.'

'No. I am going to tell everyone now.' Kevin walked out of the dressing room, walked straight to the FA and the press and announced there and then that he was resigning. We were all in shock, we couldn't believe it. I know it was a terrible result, but Kevin was that sort of character, once he made a decision, he wasn't going to go back on his word. And that's what he did. He followed his heart and went with it.

I really enjoyed working with Kevin, and although people would say that coaching-wise Glenn Hoddle was probably better, man-management-wise I thought Kevin Keegan was in a different class.

But we had to move on. Howard Wilkinson was appointed to take temporary charge and we played our next game against Finland. That was nearly my best moment for England. I scored a late goal that would have been the match-winner in different circumstances, but it wasn't given. The ball had crossed the line, but in the days before goal-line technology we just had to take that on the chin. To score for England would have been an immensely proud moment. Howard praised my performance and said we all knew it was a goal. Obviously I was disappointed.

Howard was not a long-term choice, so it didn't count for too much that he liked my contribution. Sven-Göran Eriksson came in and I was in one squad that he chose, but after that I never seemed to get in. I mean, he had a lot of good youngsters coming through – Frank Lampard, Steven Gerrard, Beckham was already a mainstay – and I just didn't get a chance after that. It was okay. I took the view I would be better off taking more of an interest in my club career. I would probably prolong that if I didn't play international football.

I did enjoy playing for England. It gave me the opportunity to get to know players who I was more used to being up against. Stuart Pearce was such a hard opponent when I played right midfield. Dennis Wise was always a nightmare to play against. He was great to have on your team when we were on the England trips, we got on really well, but on the pitch he was a totally different character, and not someone who would give you an easy ride. He was a bit like Martin Keown could be for us. On the pitch, those guys were animals and would do anything they could to beat their opponent. Wisey was such a character, especially in the England card school. We used to play cards a lot, and we always used to clean up, beat Michael Owen and Alan Shearer and all those guys. All the Londoners always used to win the money, which was great.

It was disappointing to end up with only ten caps, but maybe it was meant to be. I could have had lots of caps with no medals. But I consider myself lucky that even if I didn't get so many caps, I've got the medals to look back on and they mean the world to me.

7

What are You Doing Here, Igors?

Being voted Player of the Year by the Arsenal Football Supporters Club in 1998 was such an honour. Dennis Bergkamp won it in 1997, and a couple of years later it was all about Thierry Henry. But it speaks volumes about the kind of club we were then that, in between those two, myself and Nigel Winterburn got our names etched onto the famous crest they had in the old days.

When I got back to pre-season Arsène said, 'I want a word with you,' and I was thinking: oh no, what's happened here? I imagined someone had written in from holiday complaining about me and I was going to get fined. He pulled me into his office, sitting me down, and he said, 'Ray, you were fantastic last year. I'm going to give you a new contract, I'm going to double your money.' I was on about £4,500–£5,000 a week, and he said, 'I'll give you £10,000 a week and you don't have to sign up for any extra years.'

I was so shocked that he wasn't going to have a go at me about the summer that I said, 'Err, Boss, can I have a think about it?' Once it sank in I realised: what's there to even think about? He's offering a double-your-money pay rise for nothing. I had been worried about the excuses I was going to have to make up for not having looked after myself over the close season, so he took me by surprise. But that was the kind of person he was. Unless you had done something really bad, he'd just let you have a good time in the summer holidays. Of course, I signed the new contract quickly and told him the next day how happy I was to do so.

We wanted to maintain the success we had enjoyed in Arsène's first full season, and 1998–99 was almost another brilliant year. We should have won the league. In truth, we were even unlucky not to win the double again, which would have been a massive feat. I don't think anyone has ever done the double-double. We were kicking ourselves really.

The FA Cup that year was packed with incident. We played Sheffield United in the fifth round and a pretty straightforward game suddenly turned into mayhem. They kicked the ball out of play as someone was injured and when it was time to restart the game I took the throw-in. I threw the ball up the line thinking it would go out so that they could recollect possession. I was just sticking to the unwritten rule. But Kanu appeared, picked up the ball and away he went. I think he thought it was a proper throw-in. It all happened so quickly. The Sheffield United players didn't react at all. Kanu turned the ball across to Marc Overmars, who ran up the other wing to score. It was bedlam. The Sheffield United players went crazy. Their manager, Steve Bruce, was going to take them off the pitch. I was trying to explain to the referee that I was trying to give the ball back and there was virtually the entire Sheffield United team surrounding me, moaning to the ref that the goal wasn't fair.

We finished the game and won 2–1 – that Overmars goal was the winner – but when the final whistle went we felt bad in the dressing room. We didn't want to win like that. Arsène Wenger offered to play the game again and that's what happened. We went through at the second time of asking without too much fuss.

By the time we got to the semi-final we were up against our big rivals Man United. It was a bit of an epic battle, which went to a replay at Villa Park. It was all set up for us late on as they had gone down to ten men and we had a last-minute penalty when Phil Neville fouled me. Peter Schmeichel saved from Dennis Bergkamp. They went on to win in extra time. Dennis didn't speak for a week after that, he was absolutely distraught, the poor soul. The lads always looked after him because he could dwell on things. 'I can't believe I missed that penalty ... You know that was the last kick of the game ...'

It was a massive blow, but we were in the middle of a superb run in the league, clawing away at Man United. Like the season before, we were unbeaten since December and felt like we could retain our title. By then we had bought Kanu and Freddie Ljungberg to add to our weaponry. We were breathing down their necks, winning game after game in the league. With three matches to go we went to White Hart Lane and beat our neighbours comfortably with some cracking goals. Two games to go we played Leeds United at Elland Road. We were drawing with a few minutes left on the clock, and Nigel Winterburn had to go off. The substitute was Nelson Vivas, a little Argentine full-back. Just after coming on he made a mistake. I'm sure Leeds would never have scored if Nigel hadn't come off, because Nigel was such a fearless defender. Nelson got caught ball-watching. Jimmy Floyd Hasselbaink seized the chance – bang! One-nil to them. It was a killer, as we lost the league by one point. I felt sorry for Nelson in the end – he never really played for us again. It seemed like Arsène couldn't trust him after that.

Talk about fine margins. We were very close in that 1999 season. The differences between us and Man United were so small. Maybe just down to luck. Fine margins can make the difference for and against you. This time it favoured Man United, who went on to win the treble while we watched a double disappear and ended up with nothing. If Dennis had scored that penalty in the last minute of the FA Cup semi-final, who knows? Then, in 2003, Ruud van Nistelrooy missed a penalty in the eighty-ninth minute, six matches into what would become our unbeaten season. So sometimes these things are just meant to be.

Although most of us felt like we didn't want to be anywhere else but Arsenal, it wasn't long before a few heads started turning. In the summer of 1999 we had our first big transfer saga. It went on for weeks, with Nicolas Anelka and his agent brothers creating a big stir. After a lot of wrangling he went off to Real Madrid. He was a tremendous young talent, and looked set to be a real star for Arsenal if he had stayed. His pace and finishing were so outstanding you could easily see why Real Madrid wanted him. You could argue his brothers advised him badly. He should have stayed with Arsène Wenger, learned his trade a bit more, matured, and then gone to Real Madrid as a more rounded talent. As players we were gutted when he left, as we knew what he brought to the team. We felt he was becoming a huge player.

The following summer we lost two more players who had been crucial to the 1997–98 success, as Marc Overmars went to Barcelona, taking Manu Petit with him as part of the deal. It's frustrating, but that's what he wanted to do. Marc got much more money at Barcelona. You couldn't hold it against him. Although you know you are losing great teammates, to be honest most players worry about themselves more than the others. Of course you are thinking about the impact it might have on the team, but, more often than not, someone else is going to step in. Unless someone almost irreplaceable like Dennis Bergkamp goes – you know that's a tough one as those talents don't come around all that often – usually you can get someone else to do the job.

We might have lost Anelka, Overmars and Petit but the brilliance of Arsène is that he found a way to get in people of the calibre of Thierry Henry, Robert Pirès and Edu to take on those roles. Football can surprise you sometimes. It turned out to be one of the best deals in Arsenal's history. By selling Anelka, who had cost next to nothing, for

£23 million, they used the money to build a superb new training ground and buy Thierry Henry. I think they even had a bit of change left over.

Thierry had worked with Arsène before at Monaco when he was a young player, so obviously the boss knew all about him. When he first turned up though, Thierry struggled. All the lads were saying we can't win the league, we need a proper goalscorer. But once he scored his first goal at Southampton, his attitude completely changed. All the confidence and belief took over. He was such an incredible athlete, with a fantastic stride, and so skilful. He wasn't the quickest over 5 yards but over 20 yards he was lightning. Once he started scoring goals he was away.

I used to sit next to him a lot, as in the dressing room we would sit according to squad number. He was 14 and I was 15. We would be next to each other at the training ground every day while we got changed. He was quiet as a mouse to start with. I used to call him Terry. He used to look back at me, I wasn't sure what he thought of that. Once he settled in we used to muck about a lot. I taught him a bit of London slang. He loved imitating it. Dog and bone, phone, and all that.

I remember once he scored a goal against Manchester City which went in off the post in a game we won. I was Man of the Match, so we were both asked to do the post-match interview in the Halfway House, the little room midway along the tunnel at Highbury. On the way I said to him, 'Thierry, this is the perfect time to say: I hit the ball and had a bit of luck off the beans on toast.' He said it live on TV. They asked him about his goal and there it was: 'Yes, I hit it well but I had some luck because the ball came off the beans on toast.' He started laughing. He looked at me and said, 'Ray told me to say that.' He loved our jokes.

There was such a great team spirit then. No bickering and picking on each other. People often used to ask what the camaraderie was like, assuming with the mix of French and English and Dutch and African and all sorts that it might not work or that there would be cliques. Obviously sometimes it took some of the new players a bit longer to adapt and they would have to start off closer to people from their own country. When Robert Pirès first came he would have to sit near the French boys as he couldn't speak English, so they would have to help him. But it was brilliant. Everybody respected where everyone else came from and the most important instinct was that we were all a team together.

Thierry took me to Niketown once. I was happy to go along with him when he invited me. I was after a couple of golf clubs. Tiger Woods was sponsored by Nike and they had some great gear. When we got there, they had roped it all off. Thierry Henry was coming so they closed this massive store. He was with his mum and I was with my missus, Jo. We walked in and he told us to go around and pick out some stuff. Anything we want. Thanks, Thierry! I had a trolley, the sort of thing you get at the supermarket, and we were filling it up with trainers and jackets, jumpers, golf clubs sticking out. In the end I had so much in my trolley I felt like a rag and bone man. Every gap had something in it. My missus said, 'Are you sure about this, Ray?' We were with Thierry, no problem.

As we got to the reception area, there was Thierry and his mum with one pair of trainers each. That was it. My trolley was overflowing with gear. The man from Nike packed it all in my car and I thought: this is unbelievable, about £3,000 worth of Nike gear. What a service! As I drove past Thierry's car I wound the window down and said, 'Thierry, what are you doing next week?'

'I'm not coming here with you!'

The next day I bought him a big magnum of champagne to say thank you but I knew he didn't drink, so he gave it back to me. He was a magic player to play with and a top guy to be around.

When I see him now he still always goes back to the David Dein story – when we got our vice-chairman to have the giggles. We were always trying to make him laugh. David had a comedy laugh, a high-pitched he-he-he, and we would often try to get him to do it. David would come into the dressing room ten minutes before kick-off to wish all the lads good luck. On one occasion he walked in, it was just after Martin had been suspended for a red card, and, having tried all sorts of things to get David to laugh, I sensed an opportunity.

Mr Dein walked around the dressing room. He sees David Seaman. 'Good luck, Safe Hands.' On to Dennis. 'Good luck, Maestro.' Then me. 'Good luck, Raymo.'

'Hello, Mr Dein, we've got a problem.'

'What's that?'

'It's Martin. He's got a three-match suspension. We've got to appeal.'

Martin was sitting there, looking like he approved of this idea.

'Mr Dein,' I went on, 'if we want to win the league we have to appeal for the ban to be at least six games . . .'

He laughed. He-he-he. Everyone was in stitches. Even Martin saw the funny side. By the time we got into the tunnel our opposition looked at us a bit nervously. What were we all chuckling about? They must have thought we were pretty confident. I think we won 5–0 that day and after every goal we were just cracking up on the pitch. He was a nice guy, David Dein, and a very important man around the club. What a fantastic laugh he had, too.

That period following the 1998 double was a strange one. We had some quality players arrive, and obviously the likes of Thierry, Robert Pirès, Kanu and Freddie Ljungberg could do magical things. But we found it hard to turn our qualities into more trophies. There were a lot of runner-up situations, which was difficult to take.

We kept finishing second in the league. On top of that, having been so close in 1999, in 2000 and 2001 we reached two cup finals that ended up being very painful. Losing the UEFA Cup in 2000 was disastrous. We played against Galatasaray and on the day we were the better team, but it went to penalties and that was a nightmare. Davor Šuker and Patrick Vieira missed. I remember someone threw a smoke bomb my way when it was my turn and I couldn't even see the goal. I just hit it. But that was the only one of ours that went in and they scored all of theirs, so we were beaten. We had a few low points around that time and no question that was one of the worst.

The one good memory I have of that UEFA Cup run is a hat-trick I scored against Werder Bremen in the quarter-finals. We had been dumped out of the Champions League and into the UEFA – now everyone expects it every season, but people forget that for the first few years under

Arsène Wenger we found it really difficult to qualify from the group stage – we took the UEFA Cup seriously. We wanted to win it. This game in Bremen was a tough match, with a spot in the semis at stake. Thierry got sent off with about half an hour to go. It was one of those where everything went for me. I was playing on the right-hand side. The first goal I hit right in the corner, in off the post. The second was a dribbly one. The third I made a strong run and just leathered it. I didn't get many hat-tricks, so that was a great moment. I think some of our fans told their German counterparts that I was known as the Romford Pelé and they were quite impressed!

Don't remind me of the 2001 FA Cup final against Liverpool. That was unbelievable really. That was the referee and linesmen's fault. We should have gone 1–0 up and seen them reduced down to ten men very early when Stéphane Henchoz got his elbow in the way on the line which prevented Thierry from scoring. It turned out that was Michael Owen's day. He was on form, our back four was getting a bit older, and they snatched it from us late on. It was a sickener. But I find I try to forget the games like that. I try not to dwell on things and let it gnaw away when we lose.

It says something about the strength of our squad at the time that we had the experience of Lauren, Kanu, Dennis Bergkamp and myself on our bench for that FA Cup final.

We needed to get back to winning ways because we knew we had it within our group to do so.

Arsène was so clever at identifying great players to come in. But there were one or two gambles that didn't quite come off. In the summer of 2000 a player turned up on trial at our pre-season tour. He was a tall centre-half. Now, Martin Keown was always worried about people coming in to steal his position. If we had a centre-half on trial, Martin would say he was useless. This big guy from Latvia, Igors Stepanovs, turned up. He was a unit, but, seriously, he was not up to standard.

A few of us were on the bench watching as he played in this trial game. Stepanovs was out there and every single pass he made, the boys started applauding, just because we knew Martin would be getting a bit steamed up by it. Dennis was sitting behind Arsène and kept doling out these compliments about this defender. 'Great header! Unbelievable tackle!' Igors kicked this one ball 20 yards away from where it was meant to go but it still went to one of our players, so we all stood up clapping. Martin's muttering, 'He's not that good.' He started to point out where he missed a tackle or a header.

That night we went for dinner and laughed about it as we were only trying wind Martin up. We all knew Igors was nowhere near the standards set by Tony Adams,

Martin and Bouldy. But Martin is such an easy target because he bites. Once someone bites it's too tempting. Dennis seldom missed a trick because Martin would kick him every day in training. He always came out with a blinder to explain it to Dennis: 'I'm just getting you ready for what you are going to face in the match.' Martin was a great player, a great character, a great winner. I think we all cared so deeply.

When we got back to the training ground at London Colney a week later we had a surprise though. Igors was sitting there. I said, 'What are you doing here, Igors?'

'They signed me. Four-year contract.'

Incredible. I mean, I'm sure there were other reasons to sign him as well, but if Dennis Bergkamp stands up and says 'what a player', Arsène would be entitled to take a bit of notice. I suppose it looked like a bargain at around £1 million.

No disrespect to anyone from the lower leagues but Igors was a yard behind us on the pitch, it was like taking my brother to training. You could see Dennis's face thinking: what have we done here? He was so slow. Our fitness trainer, Tony Colbert, used to do these in-and-out drills and it would look like Igors's legs were going one way and the rest of him was going the other. Tony couldn't stop laughing. We thought: he's signed this four-year contract but he isn't going to play, he's just a squad number.

The next thing we know, we've got the biggest injury crisis we've ever had at centre-half. The only fit centre-half we've got is Igors, and who are we playing at the weekend? Man United at Old Trafford. Going into the game, our back four looked a bit dicey really. Oleg Luzhny, Gilles Grimandi, Igors and Ashley Cole, who had to go off at half-time.

Dwight Yorke ran us ragged. Seriously, it was humiliating. They scored the first goal, and we managed to equalise. We thought: okay, we'll take that. And then all of a sudden the goals started pouring in and we were 5–1 down by half-time. There is a massive walk to the tunnel at Old Trafford and you could see Arsène was fuming. He hardly every swore or shouted but he did that day. Obviously Arsène and Sir Alex Ferguson were playing mind games in those days, so that was a big one. I remember doing the long walk to the tunnel alongside Dwight Yorke and he asked, 'Where the hell did you get that centre-half from?'

'Look, it's a long story . . .'

We sat down in the dressing room and it could've been 9–1, as David Seaman actually had a blinder in goal. Arsène starts letting off and, because he's not a swearer, it just doesn't suit him, I'm really desperate to laugh. I'm making no eye contact and I could see Pat Rice in my peripheral vision sending me a look that said: don't laugh. Whatever you do. Do. Not. Laugh. Arsène was going mad. And that was the only time in the eight years I played under him that he went crazy at half-time. He was always focused on being calm, recovering, and keeping concentrated on what we needed to do.

So we lost 6–1 and poor Igors barely played again. But the thing about it was, whenever Arsenal tried to send him on loan he didn't really fancy going. He said he loved it at Arsenal. He ended up staying four years, with just one little spell out with Arsenal's partner club Beveren in Belgium.

The summer after signing Igors, Arsène got it absolutely spot on. Sol Campbell arrived. It was amazing. We couldn't believe it. Everyone's eyebrows shot up. There wasn't even a whisper of it amongst the players. It was a real transfer coup. It was one of those situations that was so surreal that when I saw him – the guy who had been captain of Tottenham and hero to them down the road – turning up at our training ground I said, 'All right, Sol? You feeling all right? What are you doing here?'

'I want to win trophies and I want to be involved in your team.'

Sol was ambitious, he wanted to win silverware, he was always a London lad and didn't want to move, even though he had some exciting options, such as Barcelona. He wanted to stay close to home, where he knew everything, and there was only really one option: Arsenal were the team. In the Premier League at the time it was Arsenal or Man United and being from London made the difference. Chelsea only started to take off later on.

Given the rivalry between Arsenal and Tottenham, it was intense for him. I would probably never have gone to Tottenham in a million years, whatever the circumstances. I just couldn't do it. Sol had that thick skin, he felt he could handle the abuse he knew he was going to get, and he was focused on winning trophies. He certainly did that. It was a great decision.

I remember the first game he had back at White Hart Lane. How hostile! Any game there always has a different atmosphere from the normal away games, but it was extremely nasty. Their fans screamed abuse at him all through the game. It was amazing he got through it. The first tackle he made, five minutes gone – boof – he went through and took out an opponent. That caused even more of a riot. North London derbies always have edge but this one was particularly special, extra sharp. Every time he touched the ball the whole place hotted up. All the other players – and we were used to getting it as well – were left alone as there was such a focus on Sol. Generally you

162

don't worry about the crowd. You can't afford to. If you can't handle a bit of stick, it's not worth being a footballer. But I thought Sol was immense under the circumstances.

We drew the game 1–1. Afterwards, back in the dressing room, we were all complimenting Sol. Great game. Well done. What fantastic character to get through it and play so well. They hate him with a passion.

We got on the coach, ready to go, our dinner out on the tables, and all the lads sat down. Sol was in the middle, the French guys always used to sit at the front, I was near the back. The police came on the coach and wanted to talk to us. This one policeman was quite agitated, almost shouting: 'We have a major problem outside the stadium. Whatever you do, keep your heads down. Driver, whatever you do, don't stop at the little T-junction leading away from the stadium onto the High Road. We are going to close the road off. Just go left as quick as you can and get on your way.' We all looked at each other. We'd never had anything like this before.

I shouted to the boss from the back of the coach. 'Boss! Why don't we put a big sign up on the window – SOL SITS HERE! At least they can get the right window.' Wenger is a funny man, he started laughing. 'Yes, we can do that. Good idea.' It broke the tension and difficulty of the situation a little bit. When we did leave, it was lethal. Bricks flying at the windows. As the coach driver turned swiftly round the corner, all the plates laid out for our dinner went crashing. It was scary. We have been to some hostile places, like Turkey, but that was something else. Proper hatred. To come through the ranks and leave on a free transfer to join your local rivals, that was a giant decision from Sol.

He made a huge impression on our team, adding that power and leadership to our backline which was needed – he was absolutely in the mould of the great centre-backs we were used to in Tony, Bouldy and Martin. By now Bouldy had gone, and the other two were in their mid-thirties. Tony was in his last season and only managed ten appearances in the league, so by having Sol overlap with Tony there was a kind of handing over of the baton at the back.

The squad was evolving. With Pirès and Ljungberg well settled on the flanks, I found myself playing more in the centre with Patrick Vieira and Edu, who had arrived by then to give us some more flair and composure in that position. What also stood us in good stead was the one thing Arsenal had in spades: a number of top-quality strikers. As well as Thierry Henry and Dennis Bergkamp, we had a guy like Sylvain Wiltord, who was very underrated in my opinion, and Kanu, whose skills could take your breath away. The thing with Kanu was, if you kicked him he got better. He was an amazing talent in his size

14 boots. He could just turn a defender inside out. That's probably something Arsenal have found difficult to replicate in the modern times, but we were lucky to have four top-quality strikers in our armoury. In the 2001–02 season that served us well as we focused on getting out of the habit of finishing as runners-up and back to winning.

The summer before that season began I thought about leaving Arsenal. I didn't particularly want to, but out of the blue Sunderland tried to buy me. Steve Bould had gone up there in 1999, so must have mentioned me to Peter Reid, who was their manager. I respected Peter as a player so I went to meet him. I was just starting to go out with my missus and we were at Dover Street wine bar, and I thought, out of courtesy, I ought to go and see the manager of Sunderland. They were nearby in the Lancaster hotel, so I went to meet him. We had a couple of glasses of wine. He told me, 'Bouldy has told me all about you, we'd like to sign you.' He offered me double my money to go to Sunderland. I was on about £20,000 and he offered me £40,000, possibly even more if I was interested. *What?*

Peter told me the social life was great and that I would enjoy it. But I thought: I am in a special team here. I want to win more medals, not have a good time socialising. So I turned it down. Wenger knew they were after me and he gave me another £10,000 a week. That was the year I could have gone, but staying turned out to be the best decision ever. It led to the greatest times of my career.

As the 2001–02 season reached its climax we were on course to win another double. We didn't lose a game away from home that season, and clicked back into the form that propelled us to a strong finish whenever we won titles. We won twelve games in a row domestically towards the finish. That kind of run is so special, when the momentum is with you and it's like you have blinkers on, galloping down the home straight. That consistency, that drive and determination not to be beaten, would be important in the build-up to the Invincible season.

It all boiled down to a five-day period in May, two trophies on the line. Those five days were magical. First up came the FA Cup final. Normally that would be the curtain call for the English season, but for some reason – maybe because there was a World Cup coming up in Asia and they needed to finish up early – it was slipped in a week before the last weekend in the league.

We went to Cardiff to play Chelsea at the Millennium Stadium. Chelsea were just getting good then. I was marking Emmanuel Petit that day. They had Frank Lampard, Marcel Desailly, William Gallas, Gianfranco Zola, Jesper Grønkjær, Jimmy Floyd Hasselbaink, Eiður Guðjohnsen . . . they had pulled together some really good

166

players. It was a close game, lots of quality in both teams, and it couldn't have been a better moment for me to make the breakthrough.

The goals came when it got to a period in the game when to be honest we were getting a bit tired. A hot day, seventy minutes gone, and it's the end of a long, hard season. That is where the determination within your squad shines through. When no Chelsea player came to close me down I thought: I may as well have a go. What a moment.

It was only my second goal of the season. No wonder Tim Lovejoy, the Chelsea fan who was doing the commentary for Sky's Fanzone, didn't fancy me to come up with the goods. 'It's only Ray Parlour' became a catchphrase after that. Bradley Walsh, the comedian who was representing Arsenal on the Fanzone, said it was one of the most entertaining days he has ever had because of what happened. Bradley's commentary is absolutely brilliant.

After the game everybody was going mad about what Tim Lovejoy had said. We didn't know about it at the time obviously. I was laughing. He was probably right. With people like Bergkamp and Henry in the team, an opponent probably would want a chance to fall to me!

I saw Tim Lovejoy at Ian Poulter's stag do and signed a big poster for him. 'To Tim. It's only Ray Parlour.' I gave it to him and he admitted it was a great goal. He was as good as gold really.

Considering how in the final the previous year we had been 1–0 up and the better team against Liverpool before blowing it, there was a great wave of relief when we got the second. Freddie Ljungberg made such a strong run and curled a beautiful shot into the top corner. That felt like game over.

Arsène Wenger didn't want us to go overboard with the celebrations because we had such a good opportunity round the corner to win the title at Old Trafford. It all seems to happen so quickly towards the end when you finish a campaign like that, but you have to remember how tough a slog it is. Some memorable times, some low times when you have to battle through the challenges, playing poorly and people getting injured. When it is all worth it, the feeling stays with you for a long time. Winning the title at Man United's place was one of those. We were so proud of that. We had to be very strong on the night as they were after us. Their pride was stung by the idea we might win the league there.

In that run of games leading up to Old Trafford, Freddie Ljungberg was on fire, Dennis Bergkamp just used to find his runs like a laser nobody else could see. But it summed up the group that although we played without the attacking intelligence of Dennis, Thierry and Robert, who had been injured for a while, we still had the class to win the game. It was all eyes on Freddie to make the difference, as he was scoring for fun, but when his shot was saved, Sylvain Wiltord popped up to coolly finish the job.

Going back to the four strikers situation, it says it all that in the FA Cup final against Chelsea we started with Bergkamp and Henry, and four days later when we went to Manchester to win the league we started with Wiltord and Kanu. It was such an important part of the formula to have those high-quality options.

At the end of the 2002 season Tony retired. His back was causing him so much trouble. I remember one game towards the end, away at Liverpool, he woke up in the morning in our hotel and said, 'My back has gone, I can't play.'

'What? Don't you want to go and see the physios?'

'Nope. It's gone, I can't play.'

That was it, he went home. His back problems caught up with him. It felt like the end of an era. I was gutted when he left. Tony and I always got on really well. He was one of my best mates, we grew up together, even though he was a few years older than me. He looked after me. He was my room partner, and we had got used to each other's habits. He always used to wake up really early and make me a cup of tea. But after that I went on my own. I didn't really want to room with someone else.

His retirement was a sad time for the players, the fans, the club as a whole. To have a player like Tony, one of the biggest players in Arsenal's history and maybe the best skipper, call it a day wasn't easy. His body couldn't handle it, but he showed his class with a top performance in his last match, which happened to be that 2002 FA Cup final against Chelsea.

The following season, we fell short with our defence of the title and that was disappointing, but at least we kept the winning mentality going by retaining the FA Cup.

It is a competition that means a lot to me. I was lucky to play in five FA Cup finals. I won four of them. It was a big thing for my family as well. Foreign players might not have the same personal history with a competition like the FA Cup, but I had watched every FA Cup final for as long as I could remember. Every single one. For most players to play in one or two means you have done very well. In 1993 to play the first one was a real honour. In 1998 I was Man of the Match. In 2001 I was a sub, got on at the end, and we lost, so it wasn't a great one for me. Then to score a special goal in 2002 topped the lot. In 2003 against Southampton it was a poor final won by Robert Pirès, but overall to play in five was remarkable.

Most of our foreign players understood what was required in the FA Cup. But there was a responsibility on those of us who were rooted in the history of giant killings to make sure we avoided any slips against lower-level sides. Sometimes, playing the smaller opponents, that is where the team really needed the likes of myself and Martin. I remember going to Bradford once – it was a bit of a culture shock to some of our team. The dressing room was so small you could see some of the foreign players looking around with disdain. 'What is this?' Half the squad went in to change, and then they came out and the other half went in. That was how small it was. That's where frame of mind comes into it. You know Bradford will be revved up to come out at 100 miles per hour, and if you are not up for that, you will get beat.

You need that British steel at times like that. You could sense some of the others were not ready. The likes of Patrick and Thierry could dig in as well but it was not a given. Robert Pirès was not known for his tackling, so we did that for him. He was so dangerous when he had the freedom to show his skills. We had to explain things. The pitch won't be any good. It might be blowing a gale. We have to dig in, as it might be a battle more than a football match. It won't be pretty. We need to compete and our quality will shine through after that. Sometimes it works, sometimes it doesn't.

The FA Cup third round could present difficulties. We almost got knocked out in 1998. Port Vale at Highbury, some of the players took their eye off the ball, we had a replay and got through on penalties – just about. Carlisle United in 2001 we got kicked off the park. We won 1–0 and only had one shot on target. Early January, freezing, the dressing rooms are cold, and we had to make sure everyone could roll their sleeves up if necessary. We knew that the early rounds were the hardest, a test of your mettle. Once the foreign players reached that first final they appreciated it was worth taking those early rounds seriously because of the rewards you can get in May.

In 2003, we faced Sheffield United in the semi-finals and I will always remember how their manager, Neil Warnock, tried to get them fired up to put the ingredients in place for a giant killing. He never stopped shouting, 'Kick 'em! Get stuck in!' to their team. But we got stuck into them harder. He ended up moaning that we kicked them. That's the way we had to play it. Our attitude was: if you really want to play that game, we can play it just as well.

Myself, Patrick, Martin, all those sorts of players, we started steaming in and they didn't know what hit them. They thought: well, this isn't right, this isn't in the script.

But that's what we had. We had fighters. You have got to have that little bit of fight in you to use if you need it. Sometimes you don't need it and you just get on with the game. But if does start getting messy, you have got to be tough. You need that strong mentality to say, 'Right, we can't let them bully us out of the game here. We have to really stand up.'

Essentially, that came from the players. It was ingrained in us from our youth. Pat Rice used to always say, 'Make sure you win that first tackle.' That was how we were brought up. That puts everyone on the front foot, that first tackle. Whatever your job is, make sure you win your first contest. Make the first header a winning one. Make the first pass the right one. That gives you the platform for your own game and it always helps you out massively.

After we beat Neil Warnock's Sheffield United in 2003, thanks to a goal from Freddie and a wonder save from Dave Seaman, we turned our attention to another FA Cup final at Cardiff, our third in a row. I was fit to start that final but only just. To be fair, I had seven stitches in my ankle, right on the bone. Arsène Wenger asked me if I was all right to play. 'FA Cup final? Definitely.' They put a big pad on it.

My brother Jimmy was coming to the game and he got the *Racing Post* that morning. On the back of the paper the headline was 'Massage Parlour', which referred to the chances of me getting treatment during the ninety minutes. The odds were 7/2. My brother rang me and said, 'Have you seen the papers today? You are 7/2 to get injured!'

'Leave off, Jimmy. It's the cup final . . .' Still, I phoned my bookie and asked what price I was to get treatment, just to find out what was going on. My weakness was genuine. I had seven stitches in my ankle and if I got caught it would have been painful – any player would have gone down. But I didn't think any more of it. I turned my phone off. That was that. I thought: I won't call my brother back because I know what he's like. In the meantime he has told everybody, all his mates, about this bet. Francis Jeffers, who was next to me on the coach, told half of Liverpool. I don't realise this at the time.

We kick off, I was on the end of a few tackles, no problem. It got to the eightieth minute and I collided with someone, caught my stitches, and went down. The referee more or less said play on, but I was still lying on the floor. The ref came over later and asked if I wanted treatment. As Gary Lewin ran on, all my family leapt up. 'Get in there!' My mum and dad had put £20 on it. They don't even gamble. Later on the Arsenal chef said to me, quizzically, 'When you got injured all your family jumped up and celebrated.' Apparently Romford made a lot of money, and it wasn't bad going in Liverpool either.

It wasn't a classic game, but we won, and a year after Tony said goodbye with a victory in the FA Cup final, David Seaman did the same. He was captain on the day as Patrick was injured, which made it more special for old Safe Hands. He had an amazing career. Watching Petr Cech play for Arsenal recently has reminded me of how important it is to have a truly great keeper in your team. I always say you can't win the league without a top goal-keeper. In his time Dave Seaman won the league three times with Arsenal, and added plenty of cups to boot.

The club put on a celebration party at Sopwell House after the 2003 victory, a hotel and country club in St Albans, which was near our training ground. It was customary for the FA Cup to get passed around the tables at this dinner, so everyone and their families could have some time with the cup. The cup made its way to our table, where I was with my parents and my brothers, and my new girlfriend at the time. When nobody was looking I put the FA Cup down underneath the table, hidden behind a long, white tablecloth. We must have left it there for half an hour. To start with nobody noticed it was gone, but suddenly the mood changed. David Dein came over, looking concerned. 'Has anyone seen the cup?'

'No, Mr Dein, I gave it to the next table ages ago.'

He was going round, table by table, increasingly uncomfortable. A big panic was rising. The FA Cup was apparently gone. Disappeared. By now my mum has got hold of me. 'What are you doing, Ray?' My old man was cracking up. 'How funny is this?' They are all looking for the FA Cup and it's under our table.

I realised it was getting out of hand, so I had to move it somewhere. There was a scene of bedlam. I quickly retrieved the cup and tried to find a moment when everyone was distracted elsewhere to reposition it in the corner on the floor somewhere. The great FA Cup mystery was solved.

8

Warming Up with Martin

The San Siro in Milan is a special place to play football. I'd played there once when I was twenty-one, in one of my early experiences of big matches abroad. It was the 1994 European Super Cup, a head-to-head competition which was supposed to determine the best team in Europe by pitting the Champions League winners – which happened to be the legendary AC Milan team of the time – against the Cup Winners' Cup holders, which was George Graham's Arsenal.

Having drawn the first game at Highbury 0–0, we went to Milan for the second leg. We lost the game, and as it happened the crowd was fairly small because Italian football was reeling from some violence which had seen a fan stabbed and killed on the way to a game involving AC

Milan. A round of fixtures had been postponed. A bizarre thing from that trip sticks in my mind. I remember the away fans were right near the tunnel. A few of my mates were there. I could hear people shouting, 'Ray! Ray!' but one of them shouted, 'Michael!' That name came from our time at the Rush Green Social Club. The woman who ran it was going a bit doolally — her son was called Michael but she kept calling me Michael for some reason and the name stuck. It was like Trigger in *Only Fools and Horses* calling Rodney 'Dave'. So when I heard someone call out 'Michael' at the San Siro I knew it was my mates and looked round at that point. 'All right, boys?'

Almost a decade later I was back at the San Siro in circumstances that could not have been more different. From being a kid getting a taste of what European football was all about to leading Arsenal out as captain for a knife-edge, high-pressure Champions League game during the 2003–04 season.

I was lucky to skipper Arsenal a few times, and one of my greatest moments was to have the armband at Inter Milan in the Champions League. I will always remember walking out that night, it was such a proud feeling. They were a really top-quality side, very tough and had just thrashed us 3–0 at Highbury. We had no Patrick Vieira, no Dennis Bergkamp, no Lauren – which led to a reshuffle at the back, and, according to plenty of critics, no chance. We had to win to rescue our Champions League position after a terrible start left us without a victory from our opening three games.

Edu and I played centre midfield, with Freddie Ljungberg and Robert Pirès on either side, and Kanu played up front with Thierry Henry. They had a typically strong Italian-style defence, built around Fabio Cannavaro and Marco Materazzi, who went on to win the World Cup together for their country in 2006. Javier Zanetti was a legend for them in midfield and defence. Their striker Christian Vieri had, when Inter bought him, been the most expensive player in the world, and he had a frightening scoring record.

We played out of our skins and won 5–1. Our passing was so good that night. Edu alongside me was a very good footballer. We controlled the midfield, and most games that is where you win the match from – the engine room. You have to control how you attack, when to get the wide players and forward players into the game while dealing with any pressure on your defence. We played the perfect match. We went ahead and they equalised, and I was worried we would be right up against it, but once we got the third goal, thanks to some magic from Thierry, I have never seen a team crumble like it. They gave up. They were nothing like the team we had faced at Highbury when they beat us 3–0. But, then again, I don't think they expected us to be as good as we were on the night. Freddie Ljungberg, Edu and Robert Pirès scored the other goals for us in a match none of us that were there will ever forget.

It stands out in my mind not just for the result, and it was a big one, but because we had so many key players missing. Pascal Cygan played centre-back. Look at our bench – Graham Stack, Justin Hoyte, a young Gaël Clichy, Jérémie Aliadière, Michal Papadopulos . . . We had no players left! So to go to a place like the San Siro and get a result like that was spectacular. The Italians were not used to losing at home in Europe and they had the grace to give us a standing ovation. That type of recognition doesn't happen very often, so we felt amazing.

I remember walking back into the dressing room feeling ten feet tall and saying with a grin, 'I expect to be skipper next week, even if Patrick is fit!' which made the boss laugh. He said, 'What a performance.' I told him, 'It's because I was skipper, Boss, look at the way they responded!' Obviously it was nothing to do with that, it was just an unbelievable experience, to play with such style at such a prestigious place as the San Siro. With key players out, that was one of the best performances I have ever taken part in.

After the game, just as Arsène was about to say some-thing, Jens Lehmann, our new goalkeeper, who had just joined to replace David Seaman, stood up out of the blue and made a speech. He told us that he had been involved in many big games in his time but that one of his proudest moments was to be involved in this team, and that watch-ing that performance from his goal was absolutely fan-tastic. He said the spirit was second to none. Arsène was pleased. That was his teamtalk delivered right there by a new man with a big personality.

Jens was right though. He was a player who had so much fire in his belly and he recognised that there was such a strong character in our group. At the top level a success-ful team needs to have the technical side and the mental side. Jens made sure nobody was too relaxed, he was such a tough competitor. When you are following a legend who has set the highest standards, it's a big challenge. Jens had some big boots to fill taking over from David Seaman. It was a worry losing a great goalkeeper but Jens was able to tackle that. He came in with a big character – a bit of a nutcase, a great professional, and a winner.

The 2003–04 season would go down in Arsenal's his-tory as one of the most famous campaigns ever. Of course nobody knew that at the start. The team meeting before the beginning of the season was much like any other. 'Let's win the league.' That's the main message. That was always our top priority. The Champions League was important too, but the thirty-eight-game slog of the Premier League, for me, was the ultimate test. In cup competitions you only need one slice of bad luck and you are out. The league doesn't lie. Whoever comes bottom is the worst team, and the one who comes out on top is the best – simple as that.

Arsène Wenger is not best known for his defensive work but he doesn't get enough credit for the fact he built the defence that was the platform for a record-breaking achievement. It was Arsène who converted Lauren from midfield into a right-back, who promoted Ashley Cole at left-back, who inspired Sol Campbell to come, who gambled with an unknown energetic kid in Kolo Touré to partner him, who handpicked Jens as the man with the character to walk into our goal. It was Arsène who put all those talents together to make a great back four, with a strong goalkeeper behind them, and a quality shield in Gilberto Silva to protect them in midfield alongside Patrick Vieira.

Kolo was a really nice guy. When he turned up he was amazed. I think Vic Akers gave him a new pair of boots and he couldn't believe it. With any trial you would set up the team attack versus defence and put the triallist in accordingly. Kolo was in alongside Martin, who was always a good person to trial alongside as he was guaranteed to give 100 per cent. Lauren and Ashley Cole made up the back four.

Against them was Thierry and Dennis, with Robert Pirès and myself wide and Patrick Vieira in midfield. Wenger would stand in the middle of the pitch and, as he was more offensively minded, he would watch the runs. He was more interested in that movement, who was peeling off in certain directions, than anything else. So, the question was, could Kolo Touré and Martin Keown handle the runs of Thierry Henry and Dennis Bergkamp?

We started with the ball and began knocking it around. The ball got rolled to Thierry and the next minute Kolo smashed him with a properly bad tackle. Boof! Even Martin has said, 'What are you doing? Don't kick him. He's our best player!' Wenger was calling over, 'Kolo, no tackle!' Kolo said, 'Sorry, Coach.'

The two defenders swapped which striker they were marking. All of a sudden, the next ball goes in to Dennis and – boof! Dennis has gone down and Wenger is going mad. 'I said no tackle, Kolo!'

'Sorry, sorry, sorry,' says Kolo. He was only being enthusiastic.

The next ball goes in and he produces a good interception. The ball spun off and Kolo set off running after it.

All he can see is the ball, which has landed right in front of Arsène Wenger. Boof! He tackled Wenger. Our jaws dropped. Wenger was on the floor in pain. He was limping. He more or less got stretchered off. Now the triallist has taken out our two best players and the manager. 'That's it for today,' says Wenger.

We were all laughing in disbelief but poor Kolo was nearly in tears. He kept apologising. I felt really sorry for him when we got back in the dressing room. He couldn't believe what had happened and thought he had wrecked his big chance.

En route to having lunch I popped in to see Gary Lewin for some anti-inflammatories and as I walked into the medical room Arsène Wenger had a big ice pack on his ankle.

'How's your ankle, Boss?'

'It's sore, Ray.'

'Boss, I don't think he meant it. He's enthusiastic. I would be exactly the same, on trial at Arsenal, wanting it so much.'

'I know he didn't mean it. I like his desire. We sign him tomorrow.'

Kolo became part of our little team. I liked him immediately. He's a funny man. He wasn't on a lot of money to start with though, and he kept asking me to be his agent.

I said, 'How can I do your contract?' He said, 'Please can you go and see David Dein for me, get me some more money.' In the end I told him to keep playing well and then go and see Arsène Wenger, that he would sort him out. It all turned out so well and in the Invincible season he established a great partnership with Sol. He was a winner, one of Arsène's top signings.

The boss would probably say he was very lucky that when he came to Arsenal they had perhaps the best back five in all of Europe at the time. The famous back four, with Martin Keown as well, and David Seaman in goal, gave him an outstanding base. But if you look at how that defence had to evolve when age caught up with them, with players like Lauren, Sol, Kolo and Ashley emerging to take over, that was quite a transformation. Arsène showed he was able to rebuild the defence with great instincts.

Maybe it was easier to rework a defence then because automatically he had players who were more defensively minded. It's not quite so easy to find that nowadays. We had the right blend of players who could really express themselves but did not mind putting a shift in. We could make it difficult for other teams if we had to. As players we knew that when we had to force a game our way we would be sitting tight, closing off spaces and tackling hard. Then when we were steady we could go and launch ourselves more creatively again. That was more down to the mentality of the players though than the manager.

Nobody could doubt he always wanted to score goals. But that doesn't mean Arsène doesn't deserve credit for putting the right pieces in place to make an excellent defensive unit.

People often question Arsenal at set plays over the years when, particularly in the second half of Arsenal's time under Arsène Wenger, there did seem to be a softer centre. But we did practise set plays. Of course we did. What used to happen is a scout, having watched them, would have prepared a report on our upcoming opponents. Most clubs don't change their corner routines. The scout's job was to establish the different routines so we could prepare for it. I used to like man-to-man marking. I would stay with my man, and if he scored it was down to me. Over the years it started changing and zonal marking became more prominent. I could understand the point, but I preferred knowing I had to stay touch-tight and stop my man from getting away from me. That's what we used to do, and we would be told in training who was marking who at set plays. Done. Any subs would be told who to pick up if they came on.

What is also underrated with Arsène is how he managed to create three title-winning teams. He changed quite a lot between the first one in 1997–98 and the Invincible team of 2003–04. The middle one, in 2001–02, had elements from both. He had to make adjustments, so that each of them had the right balance of qualities to go out and win the league. Each of those squads worked. The new faces added different ingredients but each time the recipe was spot on.

When Arsène came out in public after we won the league in 2002 to say he had a squad he felt could go unbeaten I can't pretend I took any notice of that. Didn't even think about it. But, looking back, it certainly put more pressure on us. The thing is, his belief in the group of players we had was genuine. He honestly felt we could achieve it. He knew that even if we got injuries, we had backup. Kanu was there. Wiltord was there. Edu and myself. Martin. He had options everywhere that could do just as good a job as anyone else.

Even so, to go unbeaten is unbelievable because it is such a long, tough, gruelling season. You always have games where you play poorly. But even when we were below par we managed to get points, scraping draws or even wins out of difficult situations. That was the mentality of the team. Arsène knew how much desire and will to win there was. It wasn't just what he saw in games, but also what he observed from the day-to-day work at training. You could see in an 8 v 8 game how badly everyone wanted to win. The sliding tackles, the intensity of the running, were full on. It could just be a regular Tuesday morning session but it had this undercurrent of a pure winning mentality. Arsène knew that if you put those sixteen players together, who all had the attitude to go all out, you should have success. We had players who would never, ever, give up. If we were trailing in a game, struggling a bit, those players would give everything because there was such a hatred of losing.

Old Trafford, in only the sixth Premier League game of the 2003–04 season, showcased that sentiment big time. Manchester United were always our biggest rival. Some might say Spurs, but, for all that the north London derby means, that wasn't our biggest game in terms of deciding who wins the prizes. Chelsea were getting better back then but they weren't yet the force they would become. In my playing era, it was always Manchester United. We had to beat them. We certainly couldn't tolerate losing to them if we wanted to win the league. I remember going into the game that September, thinking: if we can get four points from our main rival we can take charge of this season.

The game exploded late on when we felt Ruud van Nistelrooy got Patrick Vieira sent off. He exaggerated to make out he had got kicked when he hadn't, and we

Boss. Arsène's ways helped me to change as a footballer and a person.

Through it all, my family have been a rock.

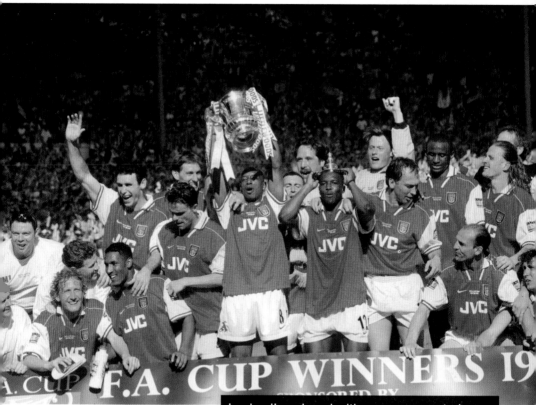

F.A. CUP WINNERS 19

Lucky. I've played with so many great players over the years. Too many to mention…

'Oh no. He's put him through. Oh, it's all right. It's only Ray Parlour . . .'

That goal against Chelsea in the FA Cup Final, 2002.

Proud. Captaining Arsenal against Inter Milan in our 5–1 victory at the San Siro.

The 2003 FA Cup with Thierry and Dennis.

Invincible. Winning the league at White Hart Lane and celebrating with the boys.

After Arsenal. David Dein presented me with an award on my return to Highbury with Middlesbrough. And I still see old friends . . .

were going mad. Then when they got a penalty in the last minute the emotion of the situation just took over. I was standing on the edge of the box thinking: we've lost this game in the last minute. And you know that's a major pointer for the whole season. I'd put my house on him scoring. Van Nistelrooy doesn't miss from the penalty spot hardly ever.

I always remember the run-up, and then all I hear is . . . BANG. The ball smashes against the crossbar and comes back out. Our reaction at the time was totally emotional. We held on until the end and when the final whistle blew we went crazy. This is a huge result for us! Even though it was only September you actually think that that point could win you the league. I saw Martin jump up all over van Nistelrooy. There were all sorts of tussles and Lauren, Ashley and myself got involved. Manchester United had a lot of winners as well and, as relieved we were, they were equally gutted, which led to the fracas at the end. You don't plan something like that. It just boils over in the heat of the moment.

Our supporters enjoyed seeing that bit of spirit at the end, that bit of anger, that bit of sticking up for your team-mates. Fans don't mind something like that as it can come across as a show of commitment. But the FA didn't see it that way, obviously. We got into a lot of trouble. Half of us were banned and fined. I got done £10,000 for that. At the time I was in the middle of a big case over my divorce settlement, and my ex-wife's lawyers were after a percentage of my earnings. That meant that, in a way, I didn't lose the whole ten grand as they would have had a chunk of it off me in any case.

With not a lot of love lost between Arsène and Sir Alex Ferguson, the atmosphere was a bit more tense than it used to be. Although there were a few flare-ups in the old days between the two clubs, we would always show up in the players' lounge for a couple of drinks. George Graham was always strict, wanting us on the coach for six o'clock, and he'd fine you if you had sloped off somewhere. Once at Old Trafford we were all sitting there on the coach at six o'clock as expected but there was no sign of George. By the time he made it to the bus he was a bit slow up the stairs because he and Fergie would get on the whiskies in the manager's room. They were good mates and whenever we played Man United George would be late back to the coach. It was nothing like that when Arsène took over.

The unbeaten run started to get longer and longer over the season, but as players we were still not too interested in that until there were about ten games to go. Our main objective was trying to win the league. Apart from Arsène I don't think anyone thought about going unbeaten.

Then the press began to go to town with it. It was like a countdown.

With nine games to go we faced Man United again at Highbury. It was another draw. Then, eight games to go, it was Liverpool. The pressure was very intense as in the previous week we had been knocked out of two cup competitions and it hurt. Man United beat us in the FA Cup semi-final, and then Chelsea shocked us in the Champions League. That one hurt. The lads really thought it was going to be our year in the Champions League. We were in such good form, and we felt we were better equipped than the teams who made the final, which were Porto and Monaco.

Losing those two cup games in quick succession knocked our confidence. We wondered: are we as good as we think we are? That Liverpool game was a pivotal one. They were ahead at half-time and we knew that if we didn't turn it around, the whole season could have easily slipped away. Thierry Henry was unplayable. He scored a hat-trick, and one of the goals was so brilliant you could almost feel Highbury shaking. That match restored our self-belief. We knew we were a good side and our focus was completely reset.

Seven games to go. Six games to go. Five games to go. The press were really cranking it up by now. But what was much more critical to us players was that we were closing in on the title and, of all places, we could win it down the road at White Hart Lane. It's always a tricky game but this one had a different atmosphere to usual. We scored two brilliant goals early on and it was hard to see how we could let it slip. It just felt like we needed to safely get to the end of the game and we would be champions.

They equalised in the last minute with a silly penalty but I didn't see the point in getting annoyed about it. We needed a draw so it didn't matter. It would have been better for the stats if we had won another game – we would have won twenty-seven and drawn eleven – but, really, the only important thing was to win the league and be unbeaten. It was mildly disappointing that they scored at the end but – you know what? – we won the league at White Hart Lane. If you are an Arsenal fan or Arsenal player, steeped in that rivalry, that's a fantastic thing to say. It was thrilling to win the league at Old Trafford in 2002, but to win it at White Hart Lane with the history of all those not-so-neighbourly emotions was something else.

The Tottenham stewards told us not to celebrate because it might be inflammatory but I remember thinking: we would celebrate here even if we won a normal league game, so I was definitely going to go for it. Thierry led the charge and we bounded down to the Arsenal fans in the corner. Asking us not to enjoy it was a silly thing to demand. Whenever and wherever you win the league, you have to celebrate. It's a long, hard season, all the ups and downs you go through, all the challenges and tests and injuries and gambles . . . So, if you win it, you celebrate wherever you are. I don't care if you're at Tottenham, at Yeovil Town, anywhere, it doesn't matter. You celebrate because it's been a big thing in your mind for months and if you get there it is such a relief.

The Tottenham fans left pretty quickly, which you would expect. We were on the pitch for quite a while cherishing the moment with our fans. I went out for a couple of days after that. I ended up in Nick Moran's flat. The actor, who had been in *Lock, Stock and Two Smoking Barrels*, is a big Arsenal fan. We went out, drinking all day and all night, and we ended up being invited back to his place. We stayed out until the early hours, me and my mates, and carried on the next day. I know we had four games left. But we had plenty of time to recover. Our next match was six days after White Hart Lane.

The schedule wasn't too hard but the pressure started to heat up. We tried to block it all out. It was time for the old cliché – one game at a time. I had enjoyed myself but then got back into training. This is where Arsène really earned his wages, because getting us to refocus was very challenging. We'd won the league. You do switch off. It only needed one of the four teams we were facing to up their game, looking to beat the champions, and for us to be below par. Arsène kept reminding us: if you do not put in the maximum, if you are not all on the ball, you are going to lose. Those games were so tricky.

Four games to go. We played Birmingham at Highbury and the game was pretty awful, one of those you would close the curtains on if it was in your back garden. Nil-nil. Nothing happened.

Three games to go. Portsmouth away. That game stands out as we got battered. Jens Lehmann got a couple of great saves and we really dug in for a 1–1 draw.

Two games to go. Another one that wasn't a classic, but we had enough in the tank to beat Fulham 1–0.

One game to go. This is it. The last game of the season and the brink of history. Even in the hotel the night before, it was difficult for us to take in how big the game was. The last time it was done was by Preston North End in 1888–89, so it wasn't exactly a common occurrence. The lads were so relaxed. Nobody was uptight as we still had that warm glow of winning the league. In hindsight that attitude was really helpful in ensuring we were not too anxious about anything.

We were playing Leicester City, who had already been relegated, but they had a go and we were losing 1–0. Of all people an ex-Arsenal trainee who came through at the same time as me, Paul Dickov, scored their goal. At half-time I remember coming in and it was one of the rare times Arsène got a bit irate with us in the dressing room. The boss stressed that this was a massive opportunity. Once we equalised shortly after half-time, when Thierry slotted in a penalty, there was only one way the game was going and the atmosphere reflected that. The sense of excited expectancy around Highbury was fantastic.

Winning the game made it even better, and I was so pleased for Patrick Vieira that he got the goal to seal such a famous day for the club. Patrick is a nice guy. He hated it the first year at Arsenal. He found it hard to settle off the pitch, even though he slotted straight in on the pitch. He became a great skipper, always up for the fight, putting his body on the line in midfield for us, and he learned how to handle the responsibility. Becoming captain wasn't a problem for him. Tony, for me, was the best skipper of all time, but Patrick was not far behind.

There was just time for one last momentous scene before the final whistle started the Invincible party for real. I was a sub that day, but my hopes of getting on had nothing on Martin Keown's. With ten appearances needed for anyone to qualify for a medal, Martin was on nine. He actually needed to make an appearance in each of those four games after winning the league at White Hart Lane, and Arsène had put him on for a couple of minutes at the end of each of the other ones.

Edu and José Antonio Reyes had already come on, and we only had one sub left to make. Time was ticking away. Martin was getting a bit twitchy. With five minutes to go Martin turned to me and asked, 'Do you think the boss will put me on?' He can get a bit forgetful, Arsène, and Martin was worried.

'Martin, go and warm up in front of him, make it obvious to him you need to get on,' I suggested.

'Ah, all right then. Good idea.'

So, off he goes. He takes his tracksuit bottoms down and warms up right in front of Arsène Wenger. The boss is going, 'Get out the way, Martin.' He can't see the game! So, Martin starts running up and down the line, they're all singing his name in the North Bank, and I think: this will be the best wind-up I've ever done. It was only a little bit of fun but I knew what kind of reaction it would get from Martin. I took my tracksuit bottoms off and, as he was clapping the fans, I sprinted behind him. He looked at me in horror.

'What are you doing, Ray?'

'I'm going on, Martin.'

'You can't! They've put two subs on already!' Now he's chasing me up and down the line, I thought he was going to kill me. I said, 'It's not my fault, the boss told me to warm up.'

'You can't! I need this for my medal!'

Anyway, I go back towards the dugout and take off my jumper, so I am now in full kit as if I am going to go on. Arsène hasn't got a clue what is happening. Martin bolts down the line – I have never seen him sprint so fast – and gets hold of Arsène. Martin virtually has him around the neck. I remember the boss saying, 'Get off, Martin!'

I thought: I have gone too far with this one.

Anyway, Martin came on for Freddie Ljungberg with three minutes to go, so all's well that ends well. He got his medal and he totally deserved it. It was his last season at the club so it was a very memorable way to draw the curtain on his Arsenal career.

After the game Arsène pulled me over and said, 'What did you say to Martin? He tried to kill me on the side of the pitch.' I told him and he thought it was hilarious. But Martin took it brilliantly in the end.

'I knew you were winding me up,' he said.

'Erm, but you had the manager round the neck . . .'

That last couple of minutes of the Leicester game was amazing for everyone associated with the club. As soon as the final whistle went I just threw myself into enjoying it. You don't really begin to appreciate the significance until a few weeks later. An unbeaten league campaign. I know other clubs have got close. Arsenal only lost once in 1991. Chelsea only lost once in 2005. But they still lost. Our players kept focused right until the end. In 1998, the game after we won the league by beating Everton, the next game we lost 4–0 at Anfield. It is easy for all your levels to drop. The fact we did stay focused was down to Arsène Wenger making sure we were able to keep our eye on the prize.

We had done well to win the league, twice in three seasons, and the unbeaten element was a sensational bonus. I think it would be very difficult to emulate.

HAVING PLAYED in the three title-winning teams in the early Wenger years – 1998, 2002 and 2004 – it's almost impossible to say which was the best team. It's a great debate to have. If I absolutely had to pick one to play one last game with, the 1998 team maybe edges it for me. Don't get me wrong, to go unbeaten is mind-blowing, and I know we didn't have Thierry Henry back in '98, but what makes it special was that it was Arsène's first full season.

Nobody expected a foreign coach to come into Arsenal and turn it around like he did. We hadn't won the league for seven years at that point, and the club was drifting, maybe even going backwards, so for that reason, with a small and fantastic squad, it was exceptional.

The other question that is almost as hard is when people ask: who is the crème de la crème of Arsenal players, the best ever? The favourites are Dennis Bergkamp and Thierry Henry, but who to pick? It's too hard. It's a toss of a coin. They are definitely one and two, whichever way round you want to go. Then Tony Adams, Liam Brady and so on come into the equation. I expect Arsène Wenger would go with Thierry, but some of the '98 boys would choose Dennis.

Thierry is a great lad and very intelligent, which is why I think he can make a manager one day. He is not short of opinions. There was a spell when he was unmarkable. For me, what Dennis did differently is that he transformed the nature of the club with his professionalism. Thierry was more of a match-winner, whereas Dennis changed the attitude of all of the English lads. Of course, Dennis was also special to play with. He could read your mind. If you were running down a blind alley, there might be only one pass on but you can't look. Dennis would read you and find you. He was such a clever player. I am sure Ian Wright and Thierry would put a lot of their goals down to Dennis and his vision.

As a game-changer for the bigger picture it is Dennis. As a game-changer on the pitch, who can forget what Thierry did against Liverpool in 2004 at the end of that terrible week when Manchester United knocked us out of the FA Cup and Chelsea beat us in the Champions League? That hat-trick was unbelievable, and without it we might not have gone on to win the title and go unbeaten.

Dennis's fear of flying is something that obviously had an impact on his career. There were games he couldn't attend and when he was our best player that was difficult at times, for him as well as the rest of us.

It became a bit of a joke really. I was always going on about the A-Team, saying, 'Give him an injection, throw him on the plane!' In the end we flew everywhere north of Watford, so it was too easy an opportunity to wind him up. Manchester, Newcastle, Stoke – we would fly. On the way home after a game we would get on the coach and have our dinner en route to the airport. Then, once we got off for the plane, Dennis would carry on by himself on the coach. After half an hour or forty minutes we'd have landed at Luton and used to ring him, knowing full well what the M1 is like.

'How are you getting on, Dennis?'

'I'm near Doncaster.'

'Ah well, I'm just getting home now.'

It was an easy wind-up but he didn't care. He just said he wasn't getting on a plane and he stuck to it. It was a terrible phobia. I was amazed he didn't get help though. In the end it was a clause in his contract, so there was no debate.

In all seriousness, we respected it. If someone has a fear that is so deep, and Marc Overmars was on the plane too when he had that bad experience with the Dutch national team, what can you do? He was a player who was so good for us we accepted it. If Dennis Bergkamp doesn't want to get on a plane when we are playing Spartak Moscow, he isn't going to get there.

I played centre-forward once at Spartak Moscow. That's how desperate we were. We lost 3–1. Dennis was the only fit centre-forward we had. A more local game he would try to get there, leaving by road a few days early. Not ideal. For the qualifying rounds we just had to leave him. He always made the effort to come to the finals, but the way the cards landed it didn't end up working out. He didn't have a great game when we lost the UEFA Cup final in Copenhagen, and when Arsenal reached the Champions League final in 2006 he never made it onto the pitch once Jens Lehmann had been sent off.

If there is one regret from that period at Arsenal when we were winning titles, it's that we never quite managed to win the Champions League. Getting knocked out by Chelsea in 2004 was a disaster. That still feels like the one that got away.

In 2001 we felt we had a great chance as well but came unstuck at Valencia. That was one of the most bitterly disappointing experiences. We had a good team then, and beat Valencia at Highbury, where I scored a screamer. It was a cagey second leg and 0–0 would have been enough. I had to come off. I had a big strapping around my thigh, and was just watching the second half unfold from the dugout. It was so nerve-racking. John Carew glanced in a header in the seventy-fifth minute and we were out on away goals. It was a real blow. We would have played Leeds in the semi-finals. They were a decent side but we felt we would have beaten them. It was all mapped out. That was our route to the final.

It is the one thing that is missing. For me the most important medal was always the Premier League but for the foreign lads, and perhaps even Arsène at the time, they really wanted that Champions League.

I had left by the time they reached the final in 2006 but there they were again going painfully close. You do need luck in those competitions. We didn't really fulfil our potential in the Champions League. Had we done so, had we made it to a final and won, it would have been the icing on the cake of most of the players' careers. Talents as great as Dennis Bergkamp and Patrick Vieira never won it.

Of course, big defeats hurt. You can't always walk off the pitch feeling okay. I try to make sure when I walk off I know that I put everything in. I can have a bad game but not for want of trying. I don't like to have those regrets. If I can walk off that pitch and accept things went wrong but I gave 100 per cent, that was the sort of player I was.

It is hard to switch off. It preys on your mind how important the game is to yourself, your teammates, the manager, the fans. It can be so dispiriting that, even when you turn up to training the next day, you are still thinking about it, still down.

That's where Arsène Wenger reacted well. If the team were really dejected after losing a big game there would be a meeting in the dressing-room area and everyone could give and listen to feedback. He would give us his view but he liked feedback from the players too. Those debates were always lively. All he wanted then was a response. Make sure you get it right next time. You can't do anything about what has gone on before but you can do something about your approach in future. At least in football the games come thick and fast and you usually get the opportunity to work a defeat through your system by winning the next game. Come out firing on all cylinders. Prove your strong mentality. Everybody has to learn to deal with off days. That proves yet again how rare it was to go unbeaten, because the off days didn't do too much damage.

Arsène was a one-off manager for me. Such a clever man with such a knack for understanding people. But he could also be a walking disaster. He would do something accidental every day. A typical example was when we were all doing a stretching exercise. One of the relaxation methods we used was to lie on our backs and raise our legs up against the wall, leaning them like that for a couple of minutes or so. Completely silent. Arsène used to do everything with us. On one occasion we were in this large room in a hotel and he put his legs up against a partition wall rather than a solid one. He went straight through it. He just rolled over and went into the other part of the room. We were supposed to be being serious and calm but it was impossible not to laugh. Arsène came back in and we had to try to be quiet but, out of the corner of your eye, you could see people sniggering.

Once we travelled up to Birmingham for an away game. On these occasions we would have our meal all set up for us to help ourselves. In your own time you go and fetch your main meal, then dessert. There were big round tables that would seat around eight people, and Arsène would sit at the back with all the staff to eat. This one day he had his main course and went up to get some dessert. He put a slice of apple pie on his plate and, as he's turned around, it has fallen off. Instead of getting anyone to come over and clear it up he hasn't even realised that it's fallen off his plate. So he's walking back through everyone with an empty plate and everyone has clocked it and is thinking: what is he doing?

He gets back to his table and sits down, picks his spoon up and tries to work out where his apple pie went. We were all trying not to laugh. I don't know how the staff on his table didn't crack up. He just shrugged and said, 'I'll have coffee instead.'

We were on tour one year, in Switzerland, and we were doing a warm-down in the swimming pool. They had pool-side cubicles. Arsène has gone in one and after a while there's no sign of him. We're all in the pool thinking: where's the manager? All of a sudden the door opens and he comes out with these Speedos on. They are the tightest-fitting Speedos I've ever seen in my life on this tall, white body. We were all sat in the pool with these baggy swimming shorts on. He got in the pool and then there was a commotion – all these lifeguards jumped in and a kid next to him was struggling and Arsène didn't even notice. Wherever he was there could be a disaster and he seemed oblivious.

9

Parlour v Parlour

I got married quite young. Too young. I had been going out with Karen from a young age, we started living together in my early twenties and had two children, Charlotte and Frankie, before tying the knot when I was twenty-five years old. Then we had our third child, Georgina. It was a relatively normal life. I was playing football a lot, going out socialising as well. Karen was looking after the children. We just didn't get on after a while, which happens. I would go out, she would be moaning. It got to the point where it didn't work. We were arguing in front of the kids, which was no good for them to see or hear. I made the decision to leave her. Nobody wants to split families up but I was so unhappy with our relationship. It had turned so sour. I had to leave.

I thought it was best they stay in the house, and I went to live on my own. I spent a few months in an apartment the other side of the M25 in Ingrave, Brentwood, before later buying a house in Herongate with my new partner, Jo. I kept things quiet and wanted to keep a low profile.

The divorce was the most stressful time I have ever had in my life. All the solicitors' meetings, letters going backwards and forwards, not seeing my children. Football helped me. It was my release from that pressure. I enjoyed going to football every morning. But then I would go home and be thinking about it all. I am sure lots of people have been through similar situations. I was lucky to have football to keep me focused on something positive.

Believe it or not, I was playing the best football of my life. I was going out a bit too much and Arsène Wenger used to warn me. 'You can't come in like that on a Tuesday or Wednesday.' But come Saturday I was ready to go, and playing out of my skin. He had to keep playing me.

That was when I met my new partner, Joanne. I wasn't looking for anyone obviously. That was the least of my concerns. But as I got to know her I found out we were quite alike, with similar interests, and I found I wanted to be around her more and more. It grew more serious and all these years later we are still together. She is my soul-mate, and the mother of my two other children, Taite and Scarlett.

The divorce became infamous. It was being heard at the highest courts of law, so what might have been a private family matter became very public. It wasn't about money for me. Financially, I thought my ex-wife was very secure. Two mortgage-free houses and a payout on top of that were already part of the settlement.

My divorce was not just well documented, it made history. It was a landmark case – the first one where future income came into the equation. It wasn't the biggest set-tlement ever, but it changed the game because, going for-ward, she would get a percentage of what I earned. The judgement more or less worked out that she would get at least a third of my future earnings.

I was thirty-one years old when the case concluded, so I knew my days on a big salary were hardly going to go on for ever.

Ours was a test case, heard in tandem with a similar claim, and all we kept hearing was about McFarlane v

McFarlane. Most people who subsequently went to court would go by Parlour v Parlour. I remember going to the horse racing at Royal Ascot when I had a horse with Ian Poulter. We all had our top hat and tails on. Bobby Davro was a couple of boxes down and he came in to say hello and said, 'What have you done to me? I am getting divorced and all I hear is Parlour v Parlour this and Parlour v Parlour that . . .'

'Bobby, I lost as well. It's not great for me either.' We were all laughing about it in the end.

I was once in a bar in Essex and a guy came up and asked me to sign a book for his boy. No problem. As we were chatting, he said to me, 'You know you are in the *Guinness Book of Records* now, you must be surprised?'

'Yeah, incredible. That 2003–04 season, to go unbeaten was amazing. I never thought we would do it.'

He let me speak for thirty seconds before coming back. 'No, I'm not talking about your football, I'm talking about your divorce.'

'Well go and get the *Guinness Book of Records* and I will sign that for you too.'

I was shocked really. My divorce kept coming up in the papers, like a reference point. As headlines go, I never thought I would feature in stories titled 'The Divorce Revolution', but there you are. I suppose it is quite common now.

My divorce cost me a lot of money but there is one thing I kept that was untouchable, and that was all my medals. I had never played football because I was motivated to make money from it. I played football because I loved it. When you go into football with nothing, you hope you will win medals. If you do that, you will get paid anyway. I wasn't the type to be driven by making more money – some players try to get a move just so they can boost their salary. With me, when Arsenal put a contract in front of me, I just signed it. I didn't even look at it. I just wanted to stay at the club.

It turned out that my time at Arsenal came to an end in the summer of 2004, just after the Invincible season, and it coincided with the divorce judgement.

I went to see Arsène. He wanted to give me another contract. In those days they didn't give the over-thirties more than a year at a time. Those were the rules. Arsène explained I would be part of it – more of a bit part, playing probably fifteen to twenty games – but he knew he wanted to play a fantastically gifted kid, Cesc Fàbregas, more. Looking back, it might have been better for my health to stay and play irregularly. But I wanted as many games as I could, as much serious involvement as I could pack into my career. I felt I could still do it every week.

I loved being a part of a successful team. I like being a regular, playing week in, week out. You reach that stage of your career when you are thirty-ish, when you wonder: am I going to play enough football now? When you get older there is a greater awareness that your career is finite, it will be over sooner than you want.

I wondered whether I would get frustrated if I didn't play a lot. I couldn't sit on the sidelines. Sometimes I might even have to be in the stands, never mind on the bench. I would end up getting fat. I'd maybe lose that edge in my training, miss the buzz of stepping into a stadium for a game that means something. I was leaning towards the idea that I would rather go down a level to make sure I played. We had a great midfield with Vieira, Gilberto, and Cesc coming through. I was always likely to only play fifteen-odd games that season.

I thought long and hard about what to do. Timing plays a part in these things too. Looking back to 1996, when Arsène arrived, that had been ideal timing for me to seize the opportunity to grow as a footballer. By the end of my time there, some people might have thought someone like me was a bit of a relic of the old school, an unlikely survivor. I still enjoyed myself, but I learned to do it at the right times. I was always friendly to every single player. But of course the atmosphere changed a lot, and I went with the change. If I didn't go with it I would have been out the door straight away when Arsène turned up in 1996. There were a few like me back then, the likes of Merse and John Hartson, who didn't last long once the Wenger revolution started. I could have easily been the next one out.

Come 2004, timing-wise there was another big factor in my life. Was it best for me to get out of the area for a while? Wherever I went it was my divorce . . . my divorce . . . my divorce. That wasn't going to be so extreme up north.

It was the hardest decision I ever made. To leave Arsenal, to leave Essex, the place where I had always lived, it was a huge step personally and professionally. I was gutted really. I wanted to stay but I was just desperate to play football every week. You always hope you won't get injured but, as you get older, you are less confident in how your body will hold up. I knew at some point my knee would give up on me.

It also meant I missed out on a testimonial at Arsenal. I had played ten years straight. Martin Keown had left the club and come back, but when all the discussions about planning a testimonial were taking place during the 2003–04 season, even though it was my turn I gave my testimonial to Martin. He knew it was the last year of his contract, he was thirty-seven and he wasn't going to sign another one. I just thought it was the right thing to do. So I said to Martin, 'You go first.' At the time I was hoping to be at Arsenal the next season. By leaving I had to let that go.

I was a bit gutted to miss out on a testimonial. It wasn't so much the financial aspect – you don't see that much of the money in the end and I was going through my divorce, so would have had an even greater chunk taken off. It was more about getting my kids on the pitch, going round and thanking the fans for all their support. Probably at the start of my career they couldn't have known how I would turn out, as I was a bit all over the place. They stuck with me when I was getting in trouble, and I hope I repaid that faith. I ended up twelfth on the all-time Arsenal appearances list and, in the more modern era, nobody has represented the club in the Premier League more times than me, which I am very proud of. I missed that opportunity to say thank you. It wasn't meant to be for me. Besides, Martin deserved that as well. I couldn't have given it to a better person.

10

You Can Take the Boy
out of Essex . . .

I went to live in Yarm. What a high street! I lived about half a mile away from the town centre, in a village called Aislaby. It was a totally different mentality up north. Nice place, relaxed. Jo came with me from Essex, and she loved it as well.

I bought my house from the defender Chris Riggott. I think he had an argument with his missus, they split up, and he went to live on his own. It was a lovely big house. I went round to see it and we did a deal there and then. What a fantastic place to live, stables in the garden, loads of space. I was there for two and a half years and I don't think I saw my neighbours ever and I only knew the postman. We had a great balance of peace and quiet, a bit of nightlife when we wanted it, and I lived bang in the middle between the training ground and the stadium. It was fifteen minutes to each of them from home.

Our daughters, Taite and Scarlett, were born down south but spent their formative years in Middlesbrough. Taite developed this twang from copying her friends at nursery and had a proper Teesside accent.

We even got some cats. I had never had a pet in my life. I turned up one day and Jo had bought two little kittens. One of them used to constantly run up and down the curtains – up one side, along the top, and back down the other – while I was watching telly. It was a nightmare. I gave that one away to my mate. A few weeks later he said, 'You know that cat you gave me, did it used to run up and down your curtains?'

'No! Course not.' I think he gave it away as well. We kept the other one, who was not as crazy.

There was a good atmosphere at the club. Some of the players were excellent – Mark Viduka was a big character, Jimmy Floyd Hasselbaink was a great pro, Gareth Southgate and Mark Schwarzer in goal were well respected, George Boateng was a very honest player, Gaizka Mendieta was a talent, although he wanted to play more than he did, Bolo Zenden . . . McClaren had a base of really good experienced players, with youngsters like Stewart Downing and Lee Cattermole coming through the ranks. It was a decent squad. I decided to really give it a go for the next couple of years and hoped we could be successful.

My first match was a derby at the Riverside against Newcastle. That was a lively way to start the season. Alan Shearer got a penalty for them quite late, but we responded even later as Jimmy Floyd Hasselbaink equalised in the ninetieth minute. It definitely gave some of us new boys a flavour of what playing football for a club in that part of the world was all about.

My second game for Middlesbrough took me, of all places, back to Highbury. In some ways that was the hardest game I ever played in. It was a very weird moment going back to my old stadium and going in the away dressing room. I think I walked straight past and headed for the home dressing room for a second before I realised. I got a great reception from the Highbury crowd as I came out. David Dein gave me a commemorative trophy, to say thanks for the time I had been at Arsenal, and it was emotional to be back at a place that was so special to me.

As for the game, it was a bit awkward really, as Arsenal were on their long unbeaten run and I had been a part of that, and I wanted them to keep it going, but obviously I was going to give my all for Middlesbrough that day. We went

3–1 up, which was unexpected to say the least. Were we going to be the ones to stop their all-important unbeaten run? All of a sudden they clicked through the gears. Arsenal could do that, as everyone knows. José Antonio Reyes, Robert Pirès, Dennis Bergkamp and Thierry Henry blew us away late in the second half. Arsenal ended up winning 5–3. So, on the day I was disappointed that we lost because I was playing for Middlesbrough, but I was pleased that Arsenal beat us because the run continued. I was delighted to see that they went on to go undefeated for forty-nine games.

I liked Steve McClaren and got on really well with him. I found training at Boro with Steve was different from at Arsenal with Arsène. It was tougher physically. We didn't have as much of the ball as when I was at Arsenal. We had to defend better. That was okay, I could do that. The lads were great and we were optimistic about having a strong season. The previous year, Boro had won the League Cup, their first-ever major honour, and that meant European football, which brought a buzz around the club.

That was part of the attraction for some of the new signings, the feeling the club was going places. But Steve still had his work cut out with some of the more experienced players who had seen and done a lot already in their careers. One funny story I remember came about after we had lost a game, and the manager came in on Monday and started to tick us off. The players were going out a lot. Obviously it's a smaller environment and the manager got to hear about it. He said, 'All I have heard all weekend is my phone going off with text messages telling me he's been here, you've been there. What have you got to say for yourselves?' Mark Viduka, who was quite a funny man, put his hand up and said, 'Boss, why don't you just turn your phone off?' We all started laughing when he was trying to tell us off. It was hilarious. I thought: oh, my God. Steve does not get it. Believe it or not, Mark wasn't even trying to be funny. He was serious. But the rest of us were in stitches.

Steve was a good coach, did his homework. At Middlesbrough we always got a big sheet of paper with a load of detail about who we were playing against. I thought: what do you need this for? You should know all about your opponents. If you are a professional footballer you should watch that much football that you know about the other teams and their strengths and weaknesses. If I am playing against Man United, I don't need a sheet of paper telling me about the player I am up against. I used to muck about. 'Look, it's got my player's favourite CD on this week's sheet. Favourite film . . .'

Some players would look at the paper and it could affect their confidence. 'Look at him, he's quick, scores goals, can cross with either foot.' They would crap themselves! So sometimes it didn't help.

I spent a bit of time with the youngsters, who were great. I was like their dad. They were all teenagers and I was in my thirties. They enjoyed all the banter that I brought up from London and asked me lots of questions about how things were at Arsenal. A lot of the older lads, like Gareth Southgate, sat over the other side, were a bit more serious, and I thought: I am going to have more fun with the youngsters.

I love my horse racing. I had horses up there with Ian Poulter, at Thirsk. Kevin Ryan was our trainer and it was fascinating to be able to take a more active role in the sport. If you live near Yorkshire there is a race meeting every day. Within about an hour you could go racing. I went on a regular basis in the afternoons. One day I was getting suited and booted, putting my tie on, and all the youngsters came up to me, full of curiosity. 'Where are you going today?'

'I am going racing, to York, the Ebor Festival, one of the best meetings in England.'

One of the lads piped up, 'I've never been racing.'

'Lads, I will do you a favour today. I will take you and look after you if you want to come.'

A handful of them did, the likes of Stewart Downing and Lee Cattermole. I told them to get their suits and ties on and meet me in Yarm High Street in an hour. I sorted out their tickets, and we arranged a big car. We got to the track and the boys were staring, wide-eyed. None of them had ever been racing in their lives and they walked in, everyone dressed up, the women looking so smart, we had a few glasses of champagne. They had a few bets, a couple of winners. They couldn't believe it, what a day.

A few weeks later they were still talking about it and I told them I was off racing again. They were falling over themselves to come along. But this time it was Sedgefield. If the Ebor at York is like going to the Premier League, Sedgefield was like going to a League Two side. Totally different. People with flat caps and jeans on. Diehard racing people.

I told the lads to go and get changed but that I would meet them there this time as I had to head off early to see some of the trainers and pick up some tips. I left tickets for them on the door at Sedgefield and waited at the bar next to the turnstiles where they would come in. I was in a tatty pair of jeans, old jacket, racing hat on, all scruffy, waiting for the scene when my young teammates showed up.

They walked through with their suits on and looked agog when they realised this was nothing like the last one. No champagne, no women in dresses. I was at the bar and they said, 'What have you done to us? What is this?'

'This is proper racing,' I told them. 'Last time you went to upper-class racing but this is working-class racing. Real racing.' They watched one race but felt so out of place they left immediately after. It was good fun, even if they weren't so up for it.

It was a successful time at the club and on and off the field I really enjoyed my time at Boro. We came seventh in the league in my first year there, the highest finish the club had managed in forty years. The UEFA Cup went quite well too. We eliminated Lazio, which was a feather in Boro's cap, and reached the last sixteen before going out to Sporting Lisbon. A lot of top teams were a little bit wary of us. We would always give them a challenging game, especially at the Riverside. Anyone who beat us there had to earn their victory.

In my second season we went on an incredible European run. We had games where we came back from the dead, goals flying in, heroic performances all over the place. In the knock-out stage we beat Stuttgart, AS Roma, Basel and Steaua Bucharest. The quarter-finals and semi-finals were mad. Both times we were 3–0 down on aggregate and rallied to score four times to win 4–3. They were crazy results, the kind of thing that doesn't happen very often for any club, and certainly put Middlesbrough on the map that season. The Italian striker Massimo Maccarone came up with the goods to breathe hope into situations that seemed impossible.

For a little club like Middlesbrough, what happened that season in Europe was amazing. Some of the teams we beat were surprised by us. We had a really good squad and the UEFA Cup inspired everyone. I was injured for a fair amount of the season so spent quite a lot of it watching from the stands, but it was still a sensational thing to witness. I was injured from September to January. That was the longest time I ever had out. I had a couple of operations when I was younger to take a lot of cartilage out of my knee, but you end up like an old car, things just start to go wrong. The wear and tear in my knee was too much by that point. It's strange. One of the attractions of going to Middlesbrough was the prospect of playing every week, but, when my knee gave way on me, maybe that was a problem in the end.

What I was watching was topsy-turvy. Although Europe was outstanding, in the league we were mediocre. It was a bizarre season in a way because it was so turbulent. The atmosphere was very erratic. Obviously the fans were thrilled with the European run, but on the other side of the coin, when things got bad it got a bit nasty. I remember one game where we lost 4–0 at home to Aston Villa and one of the fans ran onto the pitch and chucked his season ticket at the manager in disgust.

Three days after finishing a not particularly respectable fourteenth in the league we headed to Eindhoven for the UEFA Cup final against Sevilla. I was on the bench for the final. Steve McClaren went with James Morrison, who had played quite a lot of matches during the run. But I did feel experience could count on the big occasion – I had played in lots of finals. Morrison was a great young player but he froze on the night. He was just nineteen and it was a big stage. It was too much for him.

I respected that Steve had to make that decision but it ended up being a tough one for Morrison, a huge game against Sevilla. We ended up going down 4–0, and I remember Steve McClaren asked me to warm up late on. '*What?*' I didn't want to go on at 4–0 down really. I wasn't going to change the game now, was I? By then I was a holding midfielder, not an attacking one, so it seemed pretty futile. It was a really poor game, but all credit to Middlesbrough for getting there. For a small town in England to get to a European final meant a lot to everybody.

The mentality of the club overall at that time was very positive. The chairman, Steve Gibson, worked wonders, put loads of money into his hometown club, and he was a manager's dream as a chairman. Any manager would have half a chance with him, as he would always back you and stick by you and do things the right way.

Middlesbrough was a good chapter. Happy times. The ending, however, was very sudden. Although I had signed a deal for three seasons I didn't end up seeing that through. The third season led to a quite significant change. Steve McClaren left to become England manager in the summer. He had been linked to it for quite a long time, and I had always said to him, 'Boss, let me know when you are getting it. Give me a steer. I want to put a bet on you!'

'Oh, I can't tell you,' he'd reply, waving me away. It wasn't serious but it was fun to muck about with him like that.

Gareth Southgate got the job at Middlesbrough. He was a teammate, I got on really well with Gareth, but he tried to change overnight. It was really weird. Suddenly I felt: I can't talk to you like a player any more, how I used to.

It didn't help that I came out with a dodgy joke that didn't go down very well. It was in a team meeting soon after he took over. He was manager now. One of the coaches was Steve Harrison, who was so funny. His dad was a comedian and he was a great lad. We used to tell

225

each other jokes at training and we had a real good under-standing. So, when Gareth got the job, he wanted a big meeting in this video room and we had everybody there. We had the launderette women, the chefs, everybody just crammed in this room and I was sitting right at the back with Steve Harrison and Lee Cattermole.

Gareth's nickname was Gate, but that was about to be discarded. He comes in with his big introductory speech: 'Right, I'm the boss now. I'm the gaffer. I know it's going to be awkward for a lot of you, but I don't want you to call me Gate any more. I won't hold it against you if you call me Gareth, but from now on I want you to call me Boss or Gaffer.' I was sitting next to Steve Harrison, just listening, looking at each other. And I don't know what came out of me, but I went, 'What about Big Nose?'

It all went quiet. Steve Harrison started laughing even though he was the coach. Lee Cattermole's pinched me. Everyone heard it but there was no reaction at all from Gareth, not the tiniest hint of anything. He just clocked me and carried on talking.

He said, 'We are going to move this club forward and this is what I want to do . . .' It was the usual spiel but I just remember thinking: how is he going to do that? We are going to need a new team if he wants to go for serious trophies.

I don't know whether he was planning to change it anyway but he put me in the reserves. I didn't expect it. I went to go with the first team and was told, 'No, you are with the reserves today.' From that team meeting onwards he just wasn't having me.

One day he put me in the team for a reserve match on a Tuesday night away to Blackburn Rovers. I was thirty-three. Do I really need to travel to play in the reserves in the pissing rain? But I double-bluffed it. I imagine he thought my attitude would stink but I thought: right, I am going to prepare for this like I would for a cup final. So the night before, I went home and told my missus, I am going to have the same routine as if I was getting ready for a big game. Exactly the same. Food, rest, everything. I could have just tossed it off, and not bothered. It was an evening kick-off, I had my pre-match meal properly. You know when you are going in the reserves they don't feed you.

I got on the coach. 'Right, lads, you up for today?' All the youngsters were going, 'Jesus, he's up for it!' We got to Blackburn, it's raining and in the dressing room before the game, I geed up the team. I acted like a proper captain. I was ready to go out there and have the game of my life. I was slide-tackling people, setting goals up, we ended up winning 3–2. The few old blokes who were there spectating gave me a standing ovation at the end. They couldn't believe what they have just seen. A 33-year-old running around like that, as if it was my first-ever game. And all the youngsters after the game were impressed, saying, 'You were superb, and really helped us.'

I remember Malcolm Crosby, a wise old football man, was there. He had come to watch me before reporting back to the manager. After the game, he told me I had been different class. At that time, Middlesbrough were losing games. The first team were on a poor run, and I said to Malcolm that I expected to be in training with the first team tomorrow, make sure it happens. I'd proved my point. I didn't come here and sulk. I made it clear I wanted to be back and involved and competing to play in the first team.

It was a late night. I got back in the early hours of the morning from Blackburn. The following day I went to go to training nice and bright and early, expecting to be back in the first team. Normally I'd probably do a warm-down, but I figured I was back in the reckoning. Gareth said, 'You are still in the reserves.' That really surprised me. So that was that then. I said, 'Right, I'm leaving.'

You are not suited to everyone and I was getting old, I get that. Maybe the 'Big Nose' thing was the last nail in the coffin for me. But I didn't expect that response. I thought he would laugh. Obviously he didn't as he was trying to put a marker down, as if to say: you can't mess with me.

We did a deal where I would get half of the remaining money on my contract. I had six months left, they gave me three months' salary, and I left. I brought my family back to London.

I have no regrets about the time I spent at Middlesbrough, but I do sometimes wonder whether, if I had made a different decision and stayed at Highbury, I might have reached that magic 500-game mark. That would have been a massive milestone. I was on 466 games for Arsenal when I left. I wanted more games, and I played forty-one times in my first season with Middlesbrough, and sixty games in total before I left. Arsène knew that forty-one games in one season was overloading my body at that stage, which is probably why my knee took the hit soon afterwards. He would have probably nursed me more carefully, with the fifteen-odd games a season he had in mind, and I might have had another couple of years at Arsenal. Would I have got that extra thirty-four appearances to reach 500 if I had stayed? Probably.

11

To Hull and Back

January 2007. What do I do? I didn't have a house any more in Essex since upping sticks and moving to Middlesbrough. Approaching my thirty-fourth birthday, for the first time since I was a kid I didn't have a club either. What now? I am not bad at organising myself, so I got a house for the family, getting Jo and our two little girls, Taite and Scarlett, settled. As far as football was concerned, obviously the phone call went in to Arsène Wenger. He has always been brilliant like that. He will let former players come back and train.

'Boss, would you mind if I come down to London Colney because I want to try to keep fit, get my football brain ticking over?'

'No problem whatsoever, Ray.'

I think he liked me going back. I went to the dressing room area and suddenly all the lads saw me, all the staff I knew from before, and I could slot straight into the life of the training ground. Arsène knew I could bring a blend of camaraderie and a hard-work ethic. I loved going back, I really did. No disrespect to Middlesbrough, but once I got training, the levels were so high I started getting so sharp, was improving so much, and in fact maybe Arsène was looking at me and wondering about signing me again, like he did with a few other former players. That happened with Sol Campbell, Jens Lehmann and Thierry Henry from my time, who all went back to train and ended up getting into the squad for a second spell with Arsenal. And there were some injuries, so you never know . . .

As it happened, something quite different turned up. Steve Bould was Arsenal's youth-team manager at that time, but he used to watch a few first-team sessions and he phoned his mate Steve Parkin, who was first-team coach up at Hull City, and told him that I was working really hard, training well, and not doing anything at the weekends. And that's when I got a phone call from Phil Brown, who was the manager at Hull. 'What are you doing at the weekends, Ray?'

'Nothing.'

'Do you want to play football?'

'Yeah, I'd love to . . . But how will it work?'

With all respect to Hull as a club or a place to live, I had just brought my family back from the north-east and I wasn't going to disrupt them once again – possibly only for a short time given my age – and I was reluctant to go up to live on my own, because I knew I would end up going out and probably doing the wrong things. I explained it to Phil. 'I would love to play at the weekends but the only problem I have is the prospect of moving to Hull.'

'What about we come to an arrangement? If Arsène Wenger doesn't mind you training Mondays to Thursdays, we can get a car to pick you up for Friday, take you to the training session, you train with the lads on Friday morning, play the game Saturday and then you go straight back home?'

'That sounds good.'

So that's what happened. They gave me a contract. I said, 'I'm going to be fair on you guys as well: you only pay me if I play the games. If I get injured training for Arsenal, I don't want any money, simple as that. That's how it works.'

It was quite funny – imagine turning up Friday morning. I used to wind them up. 'All right, lads? Yeah, I've been in Spain this week, beautiful weather out there, fantastic . . .' And they grimaced as they told me they had done two double days of training in Hull.

But really, in the back of my mind, I knew I was training hard and fighting fit. I didn't muck about and take it for granted that I could have had more or less two days off in the week. I trained every day and it was all about performances. I knew that the first thing they were going to look at is whether I was putting the effort in. On some occasions, I was actually training too hard with Arsenal. There were times when the Premier League schedule meant I was in the training session with Arsène Wenger when, if their preparation was geared towards a game on Sunday or Monday, Thursday was a particularly tough day. I still had a game Saturday but I would mess Arsenal's numbers up if I pulled out, and I had to keep training as hard as everybody else because that is what is demanded of you. I was knackered. Afterwards I sometimes mentioned it to Arsène. 'Boss, do you realise I have got a game Saturday?'

'Oh, Ray, I forgot. You should have told me,'

But I still managed to play all right come the Saturday game.

Being back around the Arsenal dressing room, one thing that struck me straight away was the friction. That wasn't the best time during Arsène Wenger's era, there were a few personalities that didn't get along or maybe were not as good-natured and team-orientated as what I had been used to.

I was in a bit of a predicament – I would talk to the staff about it sometimes, but I would never say anything to the players, because it wasn't my place to do that. I was not employed by Arsenal Football Club any more. I didn't have that status. I thought it was a little disrespectful for me to just walk back in the dressing room and start having a go at players, when I'm nothing to do with the club apart from being privileged enough to join in at training. I'm sure they would have said exactly that back to me: you are nothing to do with Arsenal any more. You are training with us, but you are nothing to do with the club.

Don't get me wrong, I was sorely tempted. I could just see the different cliques, and that not everybody was pulling in the same direction. That didn't exist in the Arsenal dressing rooms I had been in before. You need everyone to buy into the same ideas, you need to know everyone will cover everyone else's back, even if you are not all going to be best mates.

Cesc Fàbregas was not talking to William Gallas. Two important players in the dressing room. They didn't like each other. They weren't getting along and I don't think you can have that. You have got to have respect for each other, and when you are on that football field, if your mate is under pressure, in trouble, you have got to help him out. When you don't get on, is he going to help you out as much as he should do? I just thought the atmosphere wasn't right, but it wasn't in my best interests to say something because I'd be butting in when it wasn't my place.

I had been in happy dressing rooms at Arsenal, under both George Graham and Arsène Wenger, and again at Middlesbrough and at Hull. So this was the first time I had witnessed a bad dressing room and it was a bit of a shock, if I am honest. If you are going to be successful, everybody in that dressing room needs to understand a certain way of doing things. Look, not everybody gets on. But you have to communicate with each other and I saw no communication. I mean, one day I saw Fàbregas and Gallas walk past each other like the other one didn't exist. How is that going to work with your skipper and leading midfielder? The skipper has to talk to his players, and those players have to respect their skipper.

If you have those bad times when you start losing, you desperately need everyone to stick together, as it's easy to start pointing fingers at each other. Easy excuses. It doesn't take much for someone to start with the blame game. 'It's your fault!' No. No way. That's no good at all. It's everybody's fault, for not going the right way.

That kind of bad atmosphere would never have been tolerated when we had Tony Adams, Patrick Vieira, players who were absolutely respected by fellow team members. What I saw was so disjointed. The manager knew he had to deal with it but it's not easy. Arsène doesn't like confrontation. He doesn't like it at all. He wants everything to run smoothly and perfectly. It's hard for someone to say, 'Right, you've got to like him and you've got to talk to him,' and for it to be effective. So he had to analyse it from the background and accept some players might have to move on, because the most important thing is to have a great dressing room.

In the end the situation got resolved because Arsène moved a few of those difficult players on. That's how you get rid of the problem. Emmanuel Adebayor left. Gallas left. Arsène knew the ones who were causing problems. That's what you have to do sometimes as a manager.

Meanwhile, on my weekends, Hull were in a relegation battle in the Championship. It was a different kind of situation from what I was used to experiencing in my career, but I knew what it was like to play under pressure and have a lot at stake, and was ready to lend whatever qualities I could to their cause. They had also just signed Dean Windass, a Hull legend and a big character, to help make a difference.

The first match I played up in Hull at the KC Stadium was amazing. Birmingham were the visitors, top of the Championship. I set up a goal for Dean Windass and we beat them 2–0. The players couldn't believe it. The fans couldn't believe it. Up to that point there were times when the ball was like a hot potato for them. They didn't seem to want the ball. I said, 'Lads, relax. If you are in trouble, pass it back to us in midfield.'

It was a different level. I remember once winning the ball in midfield and the winger had gone past the opposition full-back, so I passed it 10 yards in front of him to run onto. We were taught to do that at Arsenal. He just stayed there, though, and the ball went out for a throw-in. Everybody thought it was a bad pass! Afterwards I had to explain it to him, show him how he would have 10 yards on his opponent and he would be through if he ran on to receive the pass in space. 'Oh yeah!'

But going down to the Championship was brilliant. The press after the Birmingham game all wanted to speak to Dean and me and they seemed so curious as to what we were doing there. First question: 'Why do you want to play for Hull in a relegation battle?' I said, 'I have never played in a relegation battle in my whole life and I think it will be really exciting.' Their expressions were funny, as if they thought I must be mad. The thing was, it *was* really exciting. Every game was on edge.

It was amazing how it all panned out. Hull had some good players but they had been really short of confidence. I feel the input of myself and Dean Windass, who was fantastic, instilled much more belief in the lads. They knew they could rely on our know-how and that we wouldn't panic or be scared of the situation.

The team got so much belief from that win against Birmingham, we started beating other teams and creeping up the table. We had a good little run, winning against Preston, Luton and then a 4–0 win over Southend. Before that game I remember Dean Windass having a fry-up, while I was there with my glass of water and healthy meal. He scored a hat-trick though.

We managed to get ourselves clear of the relegation zone, but it was still tight. Leeds, who were also battling to stay in the division, were one of the teams we had to stay in front of to be safe, and it was strange the way it turned out. They went into administration and were docked ten points, which sent them tumbling to the bottom of the table. That ensured Hull would stay up. When we were safe the party atmosphere took over big time.

The last game of the season was a home match against Plymouth. The afternoon before the game, Dean and I decided to have a drink. We had stayed up already, our main aim, so it didn't feel like too much of a risk and everyone around the place was very happy. We went to Dean's local in Hull. It was a rough old pub. We were quietly watching *Soccer Saturday* on the TV as everyone else was playing, but the Championship finale was set for Sunday.

All of a sudden, a load of fans came into the pub. What's going on? It was a huge rugby league game and local derby, Hull Kingston Rovers against Hull FC. Someone told me there was bound to be a fight later. The guy next to me turned round and told me he was the hardest man in Hull. Dean and I went back to our hotel before anything kicked off. There was a wedding reception going on and I think I ended up dancing with someone's nan.

Dean knocked on my door at 11 a.m. the next day. He was up and dressed. 'Come on, mate, we've got to go,' he said.

'What are you on about? It's a three o'clock kick-off, we have got plenty of time.'

'No, it's a one o'clock kick-off. Come on!'

I jumped in the shower, got ready, no time for breakfast, missed the pre-match meal. I got to the game and I was starving. I played, but I was feeling it. We lost the Plymouth game but, because our safety was assured, nobody minded too much.

It was time to go home – or so I thought. This driver was supposed to take me back to Essex but I ended up staying in Hull. The lads invited me out to celebrate staying up. What an atmosphere. It was the first night out I had in Hull in my whole life. Everywhere we went that night it was as if we had won the Champions League. I think I ended up staying two more days.

I played fifteen games for Hull, they paid me for those fifteen games, and I'd like to think that was value for money for them, as staying in the Championship was a crucial part of the upward curve that saw them go on to be promoted the following season. Survival was so big for Phil Brown. Hull could easily have gone into League One but the magic of football is that the following year they were in the Premier League. To make it even better, that promotion was delivered by Dean Windass, with a match-winner in the play-off final.

I liked Phil. I didn't train with him day-to-day, only really saw him on the Fridays, so it's hard to judge in too much detail compared to other managers I saw on a more regular basis. He was quite tanned-up all the time but he was a good character. He appreciated all the experience I brought, and he used to ask me about what I'd been through in my career. I think he used to try and learn things from what others had gone through in their life, from the different managers that made an impact on other people. He was just up-and-coming as a manager. He had the kind of personality that means some players were probably having him and some weren't. But what he achieved in that period at Hull was remarkable.

I nearly signed for Hull for another season, but then I would have had to move up there and, at that time of my life, I didn't want to drag everyone across the country. Leyton Orient and Southend were options closer to home. I met both of their managers to see how things might work.

I still wanted a game. I couldn't let go of the bug of playing. I was going to be thirty-five next birthday, so I probably couldn't manage three games a week, but Saturdays? No problem. Then you can recover during the week and be ready for the following weekend. The manager of Southend was Steve Tilson, but whether he thought I was a bit of a threat to him or not I don't know. You know what it's like in management, especially at the lower levels – when something goes wrong, often one of the older pros around the place can get the job. That one didn't materialise.

I then met Martin Ling, who was manager of Leyton Orient, but he wanted me to do too much training. He asked if I could go in every day and at that time of my career I didn't want quite that much commitment. I was

241

starting to do a bit of media with an eye on the future. I tried to suggest that I could train twice a week with Orient instead of four times a week. I couldn't really train that intensively anyway by that stage. Even at Arsenal, towards the end I wasn't training every day. There wasn't any give there though, so that one didn't materialise either.

Your heart has got to be in it. You have to be absolutely 100 per cent dedicated to it and, when I thought back over my career, did I really want to be training and travelling for Boxing Day fixtures? Did I really want all those late nights back from away games hundreds of miles away, and then in the next day for a warm-down? The lower leagues are tough. It arguably gets tougher the further down you go, so I thought it through and came to the conclusion it was time for me to call it a day.

I don't think I ever actually came out and retired. There was no announcement that I was finished. I just stopped playing. That's a hard thing to do though, to acknowledge the end of the lifestyle and routine and atmosphere you have been a part of since boyhood. It is difficult to bring yourself to say: that's it. Over. I am an ex-pro.

It's weird. When you finish football, the first couple of months are a nightmare. I mean, just waking up in the morning and thinking: what am I going to do with myself today? I tried to keep fit, going down the gym.

That became a regular thing eventually, because that's just my buzz. Some players, you can tell that once they finish football they aren't going to ever train again. But I was the other way round, I loved having a run, getting out in the fresh air; and I still try and keep my fitness up. Don't get me wrong, my knees were playing me up a lot back then, there's no doubting that, and I had to manage that sensibly. It still hurts. My bad hip bothers me and my left-hand side is dodgy.

Apart from anything else, I valued that gym because part of it is just getting out of the house really, having something to get moving for in the mornings. I got talking to normal guys or women going down the gym, and started to get that bit of banter again. Believe it or not, even that was important.

Obviously it's not the same as a dressing room but, basically, if you asked me what I miss most about football I would have to say it's the banter. I was someone who loved the actual training but, behind the scenes, when you are having lunch with the lads and having a laugh, mucking about with the staff before the game, that was everything for me. I missed it. I loved every day of it. Going to away games, in the hotel, back of the coach, just having fun really, and after that ends you can feel a bit lost. That is a difficult thing to replace.

That first year was hard. You are suddenly not doing something you have done from the age of sixteen to thirty-five. That's nearly twenty years of your life. The absence of the camaraderie does take some getting used to. That was a big thing for me. Like I always said, there were a lot of working-class guys around the dressing room and we had the luck to do something we love and get to mess about and have some fun and laughter while we did it. Genuinely, they were my mates. Not just workmates but real mates. I still love to be in touch with them.

Some ex-footballers find one of the big shocks is looking after all the things that need doing rather than having them done for you. As a player you get told what to do all the time. Be there. Do this. Do that. I don't mind sorting all my own things out. I was always paying all my bills, doing my own house. I think most footballers now probably would not have a clue. How do you run a house? How do you pay for this or that? They have people to do it for them, but I made sure that I could look after everything myself so I would be in good stead when I retired. After all, you never know where your life is going to go after football.

I was never too tempted by coaching. Maybe one day I may want to do my badges, it doesn't take long to do, but then you are not guaranteed to get a job. Tony Adams used to tell me all the time, 'Do your coaching badges,' because usually when you do get a job, it's one of your mates that gets you in. They might offer you the reserves or some youth coaching. But there are so many good coaches out there who haven't got jobs. There are just not enough spaces to go around, so that was always the worry.

I have a few different things that I do now, which keep me busy. I was lucky I managed to get a break with talkSPORT. I started off doing a few bits and pieces and then that evolved into more work. If you can't play football, the next best thing is to watch it and get paid for it. Luckily enough, I got the chance to do a few games on co-commentary and really enjoyed it. That developed and I seemed to go well down that road. The first few shows were difficult, but once I began to know the ropes I felt okay. Working with Alan Brazil was fantastic, and we started the *Matchday Live* show, which has been a lot of fun and genuinely interesting for me. I get to go to matches every Saturday with the show and, as it wasn't just Arsenal, going to watch other clubs made me think a lot about the game. Being at live games keeps me in touch with that atmosphere.

Away from that I've got an events company with my good friend Jeff Binks. I enjoyed socialising as a player so it was a good sideline to get into. I also enjoy doing after-dinner speaking. It's a bit of a buzz standing up in front of a crowd. I love telling my stories and I travel up and down the country meeting all sorts of different people, having a lot of fun talking about my career, the characters I met and recounting the tales. A few years ago I got a pub, the Ferry Boat Inn, which is close to home in Essex, and that's a nice thing to be involved with too. The problem for a lot of players now is they don't know what they want to do when they finish playing. I keep myself busy with a variety of things.

What I like about my week now is that it is all different. It's not regimented, as football used to be. Now I arrange my diary and aim for a good balance of work and fun. If I want to be with the kids, I can. If I want to block out some time to play golf with my mates, I can. If I fancy popping into my local, the Rose, for a drink and a laugh with whoever is in there, I can.

It is similar to the old days, just being my normal self with anyone and everyone. When I used to go down the Rush Green Social Club it didn't matter if you were on £40,000 a week, you still put a tenner in the whip. Now I go in the Rose, I know the staff, the people in there – some will be painters and decorators, some will be safe-fitters – and everyone gets along with everyone else. In Middlesbrough, if you went down the local pub it didn't matter if you were a footballer or a coal miner, everyone would have a normal conversation.

Arsenal is still a big part of what I do. I am a supporter now, and am lucky also to be an ambassador for the club. Just to be involved and to represent Arsenal around the world is something I love. I have gone to a few countries, and when you see for yourself how much bigger the club is getting around the world it's quite amazing. When I was young we used to go to pre-season in Scandinavia, very low key, and it was a big deal when I was twenty and just starting out when we went to South Africa for some friendlies and met Nelson Mandela. I remember shaking his hand. We knew what kind of a life he had been through, what a hero, and it was a great privilege, but I can't say we had much of a conversation. I wanted to take him down the pub but I reckon he was too busy at the time.

As an ambassador I have travelled to Ethiopia, Ghana and Nigeria. To get the opportunity to go to somewhere like Ethiopia was a real eye-opener. If I used to think of Ethiopia I immediately associated it with famine. But I discovered the infrastructure in the country is getting bigger all the time. It was great to see how much they love football. People in England don't realise how important it is around the world.

I got to Addis Ababa and had to attend some events representing Arsenal. I met some fantastic kids, and had to do a local dance with all these shoulder moves. I think I just about pulled it off. There was lots of razzmatazz, music, and then we got to this place which was like someone's back garden to find a goal with a big penalty spot and they asked me if I would take some penalties for charity. The spot was miles away from where it was supposed to be, there was no pitch marked out, so I measured it out: 12 yards, away we go. All of a sudden, fifteen players turned up, the best goalkeepers from around the Ethiopian league. I am in my trainers and they asked me to take two penalties against each keeper. I said, 'I am not being funny but I don't normally take thirty penalties in a row.' You are hitting it hard and it's not the best for your muscles. About halfway through I felt my groin going, so I had to take the rest with my left foot. Then my left thigh started going.

For every penalty I missed, the local beer company, Dashen Brewery, gave £10,000 to their foundation. Luckily I missed enough penalties for them to raise £100,000 – I would have missed more had I realised. Those trips are fantastic, going around the world and meeting people and seeing new cultures. Although that dance I had to do was embarrassing.

Obviously there is nothing that can match the excitement of playing football – the best buzz ever was walking out into a stadium, going out and performing, hearing the crowd and absorbing everything involved with football. I still go over to the Arsenal on a regular basis to watch them.

Arsenal has been my life really. Of course I want them to do well. I want Arsène to be successful. It meant a lot to see him win those two FA Cups in 2014 and 2015 and get back to winning ways. Nobody deserves to win the league one more time more than him. The club have stuck by him and he has stuck by them and that is so unusual in the modern game. The future for Arsenal is bright because of their stability. Moving from Highbury to the Emirates, the new training ground, whoever takes over from Arsène owes him a lot. He can walk away a proud man from what he has achieved.

I look back on my career and can honestly say I couldn't have wished for more. Starting out in football in the era before players were under megastar scrutiny meant I was able to enjoy myself and be myself. I didn't really want all the attention anyway. Those boys scoring the goals and winning World Cups had a different experience. I was always quite down to earth. I would go in pubs after the game and have chats with supporters, but some players wouldn't do that. I tried to keep it exactly as it was when I was a kid. Just because you are a footballer doesn't mean you change.

Maybe I wasn't the most glamorous player, and wasn't in the limelight as much as some of my teammates, but I didn't mind that at all. That was perfect for me. As long as I was on that team sheet every single week, being in a successful side, that was all I wanted. I was never in the public eye like Tony Adams or Thierry Henry, but all I was interested in was playing the best I could. I can walk away from football and say that I was involved in three Premier League triumphs, five FA Cup finals.

If some people didn't rate me that highly I don't mind that either. The most important person to rate you is the manager and, luckily enough, someone as high class as Arsène Wenger really rated me for the best part of a decade.

I always say: you can't win the league with ten Thierry Henrys or ten Tony Adams. You have to have the mixture, the blend of qualities. Probably my best attribute was that I never knew when I was beaten. I gave every ounce, every game. That gave me a buzz. You know full well if you played well or not when you walk off the pitch. You should never walk off thinking: I should have done a bit more today. You have good and bad games but I believe that in every one I gave my all.

When I watch games today I try to support Arsenal the same as any other fan. But if I am down near the dugout, and sometimes I sit there, I am kicking every ball. There are times when you can't help but think: I wish I was still out there.

12

My Generation

I have a couple of suitcases of football shirts. It's my collection from those I have swapped or been given over the years, and it reminds me of the calibre of players I came up against and had the pleasure of calling teammates. I have loads from international or European games against some legends, the likes of Davor Šuker, Francesco Totti and Pavel Nedvěd. I made sure to get some from the best England players I met at club level – Steven Gerrard, Frank Lampard and Wayne Rooney. I also got some great signed ones from lads like Dennis, Thierry and Patrick. I even have some of my own shirts, the special ones from cup finals and memorable games. A lot of the time you give them away. Walking to the car park at Highbury there was always some kid who would ask for your shirt. 'Go on then, have it,' I'd say. 'But make sure you wash it!' More often than not they were smeared with Vicks and a bit grubby after a game.

I was very fortunate to play against some outstanding players in my time, and it was a tough choice to pick the best of them. This team might be a bit loaded with Man United players but, during my peak years, they were the best we played against. I decided to go for a 4-2-3-1 formation as that allowed me to get three brilliant attackers expressing themselves behind one deadly finisher.

Schmeichel

Cafu Cannavaro Maldini R. Carlos

Keane Gerrard

C. Ronaldo Cantona Giggs

Shearer

Peter Schmeichel

I played against the likes of Oliver Kahn and Gianluigi Buffon, but Schmeichel was the one who I came up against many times with Arsenal and he was a monster of a keeper. What a player to have behind your back four.

Cafu

This is a guy who played for Brazil for sixteen years, and played in three World Cup finals. He had electric energy and pace going forward, he was an all-round top-class modern full-back in his prime. He would be flying if he still played today.

Fabio Cannavaro

A terrific reader of the game. He wasn't the tallest, only 5 foot 9, well below average height for a centre-half, but he made up for that in the way he played the game with such intelligence. A leader by example, he captained Italy to win the World Cup in 2006.

Paolo Maldini

It is amazing to think he had such a long career at the top and was equally comfortable at left-back or centre-half. He was so composed he managed to play at the highest level until he was forty-one years old. That shows you how good he was. I had some memorable games against players like Marcel Desailly, Jaap Stam and Nemanja Vidić, but Maldini was a class act and has to be in.

Roberto Carlos

Maldini's versatility enables me to have both him and Roberto Carlos in my team of favourites. He had great pace and technique, that touch of Brazilian style that everybody knew about from those famous free kicks, but was a tough defender as well. I played against him at Wembley and got injured. I did my knee ligaments. He was a hard man to get past all right. Just a brilliant full-back.

Roy Keane

As a holding midfielder and a leader, he had it all. I played against Pep Guardiola and Phillip Cocu when Barcelona faced us in the Champions League and we got a chasing at Wembley. But you couldn't leave out Keane, could you?

Steven Gerrard

I toyed with including Gheorghe Hagi, who I played against in midfield in the UEFA Cup final when he was the main man for Galatasaray. As a player he always seemed to be one step ahead and was so hard to mark. But Stevie was a top-class box-to-box player. To pair him and Roy Keane in the engine room would give any team a fantastic edge. Box to box, his dynamic style and desire to make things happen were tremendous.

Cristiano Ronaldo

You have to be a bit special to get in ahead of the likes of Luís Figo and David Beckham. How can I pick a team without Cristiano Ronaldo though? He is such an unbelievable goal threat, a phenomenon in that respect. Look at his goals, too, he can deliver all different kinds – left foot, right foot, headers, poacher's goals, screamers. I would pay to watch him play.

Éric Cantona

What a charismatic player, and the impact he had was unbelievable. He was probably the best signing Fergie ever made at Man United. He was strong and had great imagination and seemed to change his team's attitude. Winning four Premier League titles in five years tells you how much impact he had in his pomp.

Ryan Giggs

I was tempted by Rivaldo for this position, but the long-evity of Giggs's career at the top level makes the difference for me. He played not far off a quarter of a century in the first team for Man United and won everything. I'd rather not think about that goal he scored against Arsenal in the last minute of the FA Cup semi-final replay, but those were his qualities right there.

Alan Shearer

The Premier League's record goalscorer, simple as that. He was an old-fashioned English forward, who just lived for smashing in goals.

NOW FOR the best I played alongside. That's going to be more of a 4-4-2, packed full of quality, and will take a bit longer.

Seaman

Dixon	Adams	Bould	Cole
Pirès	Vieira	Gascoigne	Overmars
	Bergkamp	Henry	

David Seaman

This one is very easy. He was the goalie for the majority of my Arsenal career and his statistics speak for themselves. Even before I made my debut he was calmly going about his business, not far off breaking the all-time clean sheets record in a season as Arsenal won the league in 1990–91 and only lost one game in the process. He played for the club for thirteen years, part of the success under both George and Arsène, and he was also the best in the country, winning seventy-five England caps.

He was so reliable, unflappable, and a good guy. Off the field he was quiet. David loved fishing. He used to sit at the back of the bus when we would all be playing cards in the early 1990s, the likes of Merse, John Jensen, Nigel Winterburn and so on. David would just be sitting in the corner reading his *Angling Times* with his ponytail and little tache. When he grew his ponytail, all the lads got hold of fake ponytails one day. The goalies would all go out early with Bob Wilson to train, so when we ran out after we all jogged past with these fake hair extensions flapping about, shouting, 'All right, Dave?' He was laughing. David was a good character. He was excellent to have in your dressing room as he was easy-going, whatever was happening.

Lee Dixon

It is very close between Lee and Lauren, and I was lucky to play with two such outstanding players and tough competitors. Neither of them would give an opposing winger an inch without putting everything on the line. By the time Lauren turned up I was playing more in central midfield, with Freddie Ljungberg or Robert Pirès playing wide on the right. Lauren was a very underrated player. Tough as they come.

Lee was a great servant to the club. He was twenty-three when Arsenal signed him and had already been around, playing for four different clubs up north by the time George spotted him. To end up with more than 600 appearances for Arsenal – he's fourth in the club's all-time appearances list – tells you everything you need to know about his attitude and consistency.

Combinations are important in football and Lee and I combined well. Towards the end of his career, I did a lot for Lee. I'm sure he'll admit that as well. I used to mark his man as much as him, but that's what it's all about: talking to your teammate in front of you or behind you on your side of the pitch, getting in positions that make the game easier for your team. Lee was very good at that. He was a top-class full-back and it was great to play with him. It was a nice moment at the 2002 FA Cup final when I scored that goal and Lee was a sub warming up just behind where it went in. He ran and gave me a massive hug.

He was a good golfer, an upbeat, talkative guy to have around, and it was always team first for him. He went out with us a lot in the Tuesday Club days but he wasn't as wild as some of us so didn't used to get in so many scrapes.

Tony Adams

It was hard to pick two centre-backs from Tony, Bouldy, Martin Keown and Sol Campbell. Really hard. But in truth it was always going to be Tony plus one of the others. He goes into any team, not only for his ability, but for his leadership as well. What a captain.

Even though we were such close mates, of course he gave me a bollocking when I deserved it. If I wasn't good on the pitch, he would tell me. And, in all honesty, that's the way it has to be. Everybody should be able to take criticism if it is in the interests of helping the team. Look, I'm affecting him in the game if I'm not doing my job. Tony made it clear to all of us in midfield that what we did affected the defence. Tony was right to tell us to put everything into our jobs in that way. Certain people need a kick up their backside. I was probably one of them.

As I have said, there was a time in Tony's career when he was called a donkey but he rose above that. Maybe that made him even more determined to prove people wrong. Technically, as the years went by and when Arsène encouraged a different kind of football, he improved. There were not many people who had anything other than respect for him when he had the class to not only be a great defender but smash in glorious title-winning goals as well. Once he said 'I'm going to do this better' about anything his determination was unswerving. I think that was his biggest quality, and what made him one of the best players of his generation.

I still see Tony, although not as much as I did because after football we can't see each other nearly every day any more. He has been working in Azerbaijan, which is great. I'd love to see him back involved in England again. Hopefully he will get another opportunity somewhere along the line. He wasn't too successful with Wycombe and Portsmouth, and not all top players become top managers, but I think Tony has all the attributes and the appetite to be a first-class manager.

Steve Bould

Bouldy was massively underrated. Martin pushes it very close for my dream team, and I loved the way he played and will always say he was the best man-to-man marker I have ever seen. Then there's Sol, who came in and played a huge role in making a remoulded defence the backbone of a successful team. He had leadership qualities at the back as well. But Bouldy was simply a quality defender and a much better footballer than he was given credit for. I thought the way he played, he was a Rolls-Royce of a player. He was just so comfortable on the ball. He had a good football brain, was as tough as they come as a centre-half, and a threat at both ends, which is always such a great qualify for a player in his position to have. Arsenal had this corner routine and he was the master of that little flick-on over the front post, which worked a treat.

As a lad, he really added to the dressing room, was a dream to have in your team and was so generous with the youngsters as well. As much as Tony helped my career, Bouldy was a big influence too. I enjoyed being around him and we always had a lot of fun. I have been glad to see him work his way up the coaching ranks from youth level to assisting Arsène. He has been around the club for years and it's vital to have people like that, with such a strong history of the place, being involved.

Ashley Cole

This was another tough one: how do you choose between Nigel Winterburn and Ashley Cole? Ashley came through the ranks. He got a bit of luck in his career as a youngster because he was close to going to Crystal Palace but when Sylvinho, a Brazilian player, turned out not to have the right passport, Ashley got his chance. He seized it big time. Once he got his opportunity in the Arsenal first team he never looked back.

Ashley was a phenomenal player at left-back, so tenacious, and comfortable enough on the ball to be part of such a talented triangle on the left-hand side when Thierry Henry drifted over and Robert Pirès was in his stride. Ashley would bomb up on the overlap and the three of them must have given opposing players on that flank nightmares. He proved his talent throughout his career. Winning 100 caps for England was some tally to get and that helps him to edge it over Nigel, who was also an outstanding left-back. Nigel was a bit unlucky in terms of England as he had Stuart Pearce in front of him, so it was probably harder for him to get caps.

Really, it was a shame that Ashley left Arsenal. I don't know the ins or outs of it all, but it would have been great for him to stay and play a lot longer. I know he went off to win a lot of medals at Chelsea but he was an Arsenal player through and through. He came through the youth system and you want those players to stay as long as possible. At the end it got a bit messy but as a player he deserves to be in any best XI.

Robert Pirès

It's astonishing looking back to think he struggled in his first season in the Premier League. Robert did not speak a lot of English and his first match was an eye-opener for him. We played Sunderland away, and Arsène told Robert to sit next to him on the bench and observe what was required. He sat there sighing away, shoulders sagging. I don't suppose he fancied it much at all. It was a physical old game up there. We lost 1–0 and Patrick got sent off. Welcome to England.

Robert did not know much about English life. He was lucky that he knew Patrick and Thierry and so on, but he was less physical and less able to adapt as quickly as they did. I think the first year was hard for him. I remember Arsène would do his team talk in French to Robert, and at other times, when he was speaking English, the French lads would then tell Robert what to do.

The following season was a big breakthrough though. Then we saw what he was made of, we enjoyed the best of him. What a fantastic footballer. He was so silky on the ball and one of those players who could make things happen for you with his creative runs and clever passes, and he had a great knack for arriving to score crucial goals too. He managed handy goal totals almost every season from wide midfield, and scored some absolute peaches. So he became a really important player for us for many years.

He wasn't so great at getting back and defending. But going forward he was brilliant. He linked up with Thierry so well, and Dennis was on that wavelength with them. During that first season I wasn't sure he could crack it in the Premier League but he improved so much he was voted Footballer of the Year in only his second season in England. Once he settled he was the real deal and a classic Arsène Wenger player – technical, a team man, and a good guy.

Patrick Vieira

When he first turned up he was this big, tall, gangly midfielder from France and we weren't sure what we were getting. He could get around the pitch all right with those long legs of his, but what a superb player he turned into.

I played a massive part in his first-ever game played for Arsenal – only because it was me who got injured in the first half of a match that wasn't going too well against Sheffield Wednesday . . . Patrick came on and he was fantastic straight away. I remember coming off, sitting on the bench and going, 'Whoa! He's brilliant! I am not going to play any more!' He was different class. What a debut. He came on and changed the game completely.

He was a bit homesick to start with. Then he settled, began to love it and became the Patrick we know. He began to be really happy in London, he totally bought into the English mentality, and he was a changed man. He was a different kind of midfielder to what we were used to because he was aggressive but also so technically smart in how he looked after the ball. He symbolised how we were going to start playing a different way in midfield to the George Graham days, with a bit more finesse. He could play tough, but had a great touch as well. He used to love this trick of sucking the opponent in and chipping the ball over their heads. It nearly always worked.

The style of football he played was so well suited to the Premier League. He could put his foot in but he could also pass and score goals. He was very influential in our team very quickly, and that partnership he had with Manu Petit was too much for everyone else in English football once they got going. For me, central midfield is one of the most crucial positions in football. If you can control that area of the pitch, you have a great advantage. Patrick could do that no problem. He achieved so much in a wonderful career.

Paul Gascoigne

Gazza was such a character. We all know about his ability, he was probably the biggest talent to come out of our country in his generation. I was lucky enough to play with him for England. I also played against him many times at club level, and he was such a brilliant player. Once he got running at you, you wouldn't know which way he was going to go.

That era around the 1990 World Cup, he was such a young man, but he was a dazzling player who captured the public imagination. His skill and his endeavour to just go past players were so exciting. I always say one of the best goals I've ever seen, for the importance of the game as well as the ability required, was his strike during Euro '96 in the England v Scotland game at Wembley. He flicked it over Colin Hendry's head and hit it on the volley before the ball bounced. Then there was that celebration with the boys running to him, and Alan Shearer squirting a water bottle over his face as he lay on the grass. That was Gazza all over. He always wanted to be the main man and he certainly delivered on many occasions.

He was a funny person to be around. Some of the stories were extraordinary. Francis Jeffers was at Everton with him and told me one about a parrot, which sounded like typical Gazza. He was in a restaurant and he sent his mate Jimmy Five Bellies off to get a parrot. It took about an hour by the time Jimmy Five Bellies turned up with a parrot that cost about £1,000. Gazza paid up and gave Jimmy some money on top for helping him out. He plonked this parrot on the table of this restaurant in Liverpool. It was quite a smart place, the diners had their ties on, and Gazza asked if he could get the bird out and stroke it.

Jimmy Five Bellies was sober as a judge and said, 'No, Gazza, no, no no.'

'You hold it while I stroke it.'

But, as they were trying to get hold of it, the parrot shot up in the air and flew off. Now it's divebombing everyone in this restaurant, feathers everywhere. It must have been chaos. But Gazza, the sort of guy he was, if he wanted to do something, he did it. He didn't really think these things through. Everybody thought it was mad but usually nobody ever seemed to mind Gazza's antics because he was so popular and he had such a big heart.

There was another occasion, when he was at Spurs, where he was mucking about in the car park, kicking a ball around. There was a camper van there for some reason and the ball landed on its roof. So Gazza has got some guy to walk up the ladder and crawl along the van's roof to fetch the ball. But somehow in the meantime Gazza has got hold of the keys and driven off with this guy on the roof, hanging on for dear life. They end up travelling down a main road and this guy must have been terrified. He's only gone to fetch the ball. But if Gazza tells you to go and get the ball, you go and get it. That's how it was around him.

There were so many funny stories, which makes it even more sad that he has found life after football so difficult. Obviously, he has had his problems in life, which is a great shame. With the pure talent he had, he must be the best English footballer. On footballing ability alone, the kind of player he was, a midfield of Gazza and Patrick Vieira would be in a different class.

Marc Overmars

Even before he arrived, Dennis told us about how quick Marc was and how he would score goals for us. Marc was like a breath of fresh air. Little Overmars was a very special player. That first season after he signed, 1997–98, he fitted in completely with the way we played and gave us a new dimension. We had Ian Wright and then Nicolas

Anelka, with Dennis Bergkamp in the hole working his magic. Because I was on the right but able to tuck in and help Patrick and Manu Petit in midfield, we used to say to him, 'Marc, you go and do some damage. Get involved, get in the box, set up goals and score goals.' Away he went.

Over the years Arsenal had some great players on the left-hand side, right-footers who could cut inside and drive at goal as well. He did that perfectly. The impact he had that season when we won the double for the first time under Arsène was huge. Marc scored sixteen goals that season. He was a funny little man as well. I also owe him as he was obviously the one who gave me my nickname, 'Romford Pelé'. I was gutted when he left. He walked in one day and said, 'Barcelona want me, I am leaving. It was nice knowing you.' And that was the end of that!

Dennis Bergkamp

Talent-wise, I didn't come across many like Dennis. He was a one-off player. He was an example to us all with his dedication, his search for perfection.

Dennis's golfing was a good example of how he was. The first game Dennis played was funny. We went for a game with the kitman, Vic Akers. We thought Dennis must good at everything because he's a great footballer, he has that ball–eye coordination and we were expecting he would be a natural. We were about 20-or 21-handicappers. We told Dennis to join us for a two o'clock tee-off time and when we got there Dennis was nowhere to be seen. We were at the tee ten minutes before our slot, and still no Dennis. We thought we had better give him another five minutes, but pondered whether he may have decided not to play – no big deal. We're just about to tee off and Dennis's car pulls into the car park and he gets out. He looks immaculate, like a pro, he looks fantastic. He walks up with these blinding clubs. So Vic and I thought: he's going to embarrass us.

'Dennis, you're our guest, you tee off.'

He puts his ball down on the tee, it's a nice sunny day. So he hits it down the fairway and we couldn't see it any-where. Where did it go? Dennis points to a bush 5 yards away. His next shot was wild in the other direction, he's all over the place. That first hole he must have hit thirteen shots, the next hole nine. He was so bad, he must have lost fifty balls that day. Anyway, it was pitch black when we finished and shook hands when we were done on the 18th. Dennis said, 'I really enjoyed that.' I was like, 'I didn't! I had to look for all your balls and you are going to make me late for my dinner!'

After that he wanted to come every single week and he kept every single scorecard. That's the kind of guy he was. He loved the game, so he had to master it. Next week he'd get better by ten or fifteen shots, the following week he'd get better still. Each week he was improving. All of a sudden he's taking lessons and hitting it sweet and it was unbelievable how he improved so quickly. He shot up to a 10-handicapper. He went about it with a determination and dedication to practise. He was at the driving range a lot. He just had to get good at it and of course he did.

On the pitch, Dennis had that nasty streak, which you need to have to be a top-class player. I remember him getting sent off at West Ham in an FA Cup tie with a high elbow that caught Steve Lomas in the face. Dennis was a very clever player, but he just lost the plot sometimes. You get that red mist and certain players would really irritate you.

Dennis used to leave a sly arm or foot in sometimes. You could tell when he went to do someone. Robin van Persie was similar but was he was more blatant. Dennis would look all innocent. 'Oh, sorry, it was accidental.' The referee went with him a lot because he was such a classy player, but obviously he lost it occasionally. He was a great fighter and that's what you want.

It says it all about the way Dennis is revered that they put a statue of him up outside the Emirates. Everybody loved Dennis, but he loved Arsenal too. He loved the spirit of it, and the way he could be himself. He was never going to go to any other club. Believe it or not, I think he would have been shy going into a new dressing room. I remember one season towards the end of his career, the club left it so late to sign him. He was on a rolling contract and no one knew if he was coming back or not. We were in pre-season. 'Where's Dennis?' It was ridiculous he hadn't been signed yet. We thought: what is going on? He was such a fantastic person to have around as well, obviously, as being the player he was.

It was fitting his testimonial was the first game to honour the new stadium when Arsenal moved from Highbury to the Emirates. He was the player who changed the way the club was going and really paved the way for the future.

Thierry Henry

Obviously the front two pick themselves. But even so, it wasn't as easy as you might imagine. You can make a case for Ian Wright, but where do you fit them all in? Arsenal have been lucky to have two sensational players break the all-time goalscoring record in recent memory.

I was playing the day Wrighty went past Cliff Bastin's total – a record that had stood since the 1930s. I scored in the same game, although funnily enough that one didn't get too much attention! It had been such a big thing he ended up celebrating the wrong goal, lifting up his top to show his vest with the message '179 Just Did It' on it when he equalled the record with 178. We were all saying, 'What are you doing, Wrighty?' The kind of player he was, it didn't take him long to put that right and he scored again in the same game and even went one better to bag a hat-trick.

He was such an explosive striker. I remember thinking: we won't see anyone scoring as prolifically as that again for Arsenal. And then Thierry Henry turned up. He took things to another level. When we first signed him, nobody knew how good he could be. We were just getting over the fact Nicolas Anelka had moved on – he had shown signs that he was going to be top class.

Thierry was an athlete really. He was over 6 foot, built like a 200-metres runner. You have to have skill, you have to have ability, but if you've got those physical attributes as well, it's so difficult to defend against. He could sprint and leave opponents for dead. His finishing was superb. He always opened his body out for his trademark finish off that left-hand side. It was practically unstoppable. He loved scoring goals and he enjoyed the attention that went with it as he got better and better.

He was a confidence player, he believed he had the ability, and he was very involved in the dressing-room area. He always had opinions in the meetings and he invariably came across with a good point. He was a very intelligent player.

Like Dennis, he loved to train. He would be out there practising, shooting again and again. When people look back at a footballer's career, they talk about their skill but don't see the work they do behind the scenes. They don't know how much they practise and how hard they keep trying. It's like any sport. If you don't practise, you are not going to be world number one. Tiger Woods in his prime was putting for the next two hours after a great round. Football is similar. You have to practise. Of course, you need the ability to start with, but the hours of repetition are what gives the best players the consistency to do great things on a regular basis. As well as winning everything in England, Thierry won the World Cup, the European Championship, the Champions League and La Liga. Not a bad haul, that.

I left Arsenal in 2004 and Thierry got bigger and bigger as a player. The last season at Highbury, when he came up with a brilliant goal at the Bernabéu to beat

Real Madrid, and scored to say farewell to Highbury, I was watching from the outside. But what a talent. Of course, he went on to break Wrighty's record, and take it on. In the end he surpassed it by nearly fifty goals. I doubt Thierry's record will ever be beaten, because it is unusual now for great players to stay at one club for a long period. The modern game has been blessed with some phenomenal strikers. Lionel Messi and Cristiano Ronaldo have set a different bar and, going back a bit, the Brazilian Ronaldo was an astonishing player. Thierry could be on that level.

I MIGHT not get in this team, but I wouldn't mind watching it, and I am proud to have played alongside such outstanding talent.

One other thing. The supporting cast for every team are the people who don't get the attention, but are a massive part of it all. Without the backroom staff you wouldn't be successful. No chance. The times when you feel down and they keep you going. When you need treatment at three o'clock in the afternoon to make sure you are going to be fit for Saturday, they would always be there waiting. Masseurs were always ready with the attitude of: anything we can do to help you, we will. Behind the scenes, if you get the right people, it makes a big difference, because it's not about eleven players on the pitch, it's about everybody: the coach driver, the physios, the kitmen, the chef, the whole club really.

The relationship between players and staff is so important. Footballers are the main men, no doubt about that, but in the teams I played for, we wanted everyone, all the staff, to be involved. We wanted everyone to know they played an important part and they were wanted and respected. Any team has to be like that to win. We all owe our backroom staff for everything we have in football.

Honours

Premier League winner 1998, 2002, 2004
FA Cup winner 1993, 1998, 2002, 2003
League Cup winner 1993
UEFA Cup Winners' Cup 1994

All-time Arsenal appearances (as of May 2016)

David O'Leary	722	1975–93
Tony Adams	669	1983–2002
George Armstrong	621	1962–77
Lee Dixon	619	1988–2002
Nigel Winterburn	584	1987–2000
David Seaman	564	1990–2003
Pat Rice	528	1967–80

Peter Storey	501	1965–77
John Radford	482	1964–76
Peter Simpson	478	1964–78
Bob John	470	1922–37
Ray Parlour	466	1992–2004

All-time Arsenal Premier League appearances (as of May 2016)

Ray Parlour	333
David Seaman	325
Dennis Bergkamp	315
Martin Keown	310
Lee Dixon	305
Patrick Vieira	279
Nigel Winterburn	270
Thierry Henry	258
Tony Adams	255
Kolo Touré	225

Acknowledgements

Thank you to everyone, all my teammates and all the backroom staff, who have been there throughout my career. From youth-team days until calling it a day, I am grateful to everyone at Arsenal, Middlesbrough, Hull City and England. Thanks also to Penguin Random House for the help in publishing this book, and Amy Lawrence for the hours recounting all these stories.

Cheers.

Ray.